TERRA ULTIMA

Martin Loflis

MARIA LÄHTEENMÄKI

TERRA
ULTIMA

A Short History of Finnish Lapland

OTAVA PUBLISHING COMPANY

© 2006 Maria Lähteenmäki and Otava Publishing Company

English translation: Gerard McAlester
Graphic Design: Päivi Puustinen
Layout: Keijo Pantsar
Cover illustration: Pekka Antikainen/www.leuku.fi

Printed by:
Otava Book Printing Company
Keuruu 2006

ISBN-13: 978-951-1-21099-3
ISBN-10: 951-1-21099-8

CONTENTS

INTRODUCTION

Finnish Lapland is a fascinating and many-faceted region on the northern periphery of Europe. The unspoiled countryside, the clear-flowing rivers and streams, the fells, the broad expanses of swampland and the chains of lakes are best experienced by trekking on foot or travelling by boat. Thousands of travellers have done just this over the centuries. They have poled further north along the Torne, Muonio, Ounas and Kemi Rivers, pushed through jungles of thicket to the deserted expanses of the fells. They have paused to rest in small villages or wilderness cabins, and sometimes they have been content to spend the night under the star-studded firmament. In their travel diaries they have anguished over the difficult terrain and the swarms of midges, but they have also eulogised over the peace of nature, the nightless days, the assortment of wild flowers on the fells, the herding of the reindeer and the leisurely pace of life, which in the larger villages has from time to time broken out into laughter, song and dance.

This book will make a journey into the past of Finnish Lapland. The journey begins with the time when it was still a part of Sweden. Finnish Lapland came into being when the eastern parts of the far-flung province of Swedish Lapland were annexed to the Grand Duchy of Finland, which became an autonomous part of the Russian Empire as a result of the Finnish War (1808–09) between Sweden and Russia. Finland remained under Russia until its independence in 1917. Our journey into the history of Finnish Lapland will end in modern Lapland, a haven for skiers, nature-lovers and travellers seeking exotic experiences.

Lapland is an important part of our common European history and cultural heritage. It has been an international meeting place for centuries. That is why we must acquaint ourselves with its past. It is the purpose of this book to provide a picture of Finnish Lapland that goes deeper than that offered by tourist brochures. Therefore we shall concern ourselves not only with its legends and the tales of foreign travellers but also with its social conditions, the changes in its economy and the composition of its population. This work, which beckons the reader on a journey of exploration into the history of Finnish Lapland, is also intended to be a text book for students.

Maria Lähteenmäki

1

ULTIMA THULE

THE MYTHICAL NORTH

Images of Lapland as an uninhabited, deserted wilderness have endured for a long time. But Lapland has been inhabited for thousands of years. Today there are traces in Finnish Lapland of human presence there in the Stone Age; for example, a carved wooden elk's head dating to c. 5800 BCE has been found in the region around Rovaniemi, and Stone Age relics and settlements have been found in Kemijärvi, the Inari region and Tervola. Bronze Age (c. 1500–1300 BCE) articles have been found in Sodankylä and Inari: in the former four bronze Scandinavian swords have been excavated, and in the latter bracelets and necklaces have been unearthed. The swords are thought to have been stashed away by a Scandinavian trader, while the jewellery is believed to have been hidden by a local from Inari.

The Northern Lights (Aurora Borealis) have always been a source of both fascination and fear. The Finnish name for them, *revontulet* (fox's fires), comes from the myth that a fox swished his tail so vigorously in the frozen snow that the sparks flew into the firmament. In reality, the Northern Lights are created by solar particles entering the Earth's atmosphere.

Another interpretation is that the objects were offered as sacrifices by the local people to their gods. Settlement in Finnish Lapland in the Stone and Bronze Ages was located along the rivers and by the lakes.

Iron Age (c. 1–400 CE) relics and settlements have been found in Lapland over a wider area than those dating back to the Bronze Age. The sites of the finds are located mainly along the Torne, Kemi and Ounas Rivers. For example, there was an iron smeltery in Kemijärvi, and two sabre-like iron weapons have been found in Savukoski. Their shape would indicate that they had made their way to the north from the Black Sea area. Iron Age objects and graves have also been excavated in Tornio and Ylitornio. The earliest travellers to Lapland were nomadic hunters and fishers, but in the Iron Age there are also traces of Saami settlement. Objects of the same kind as those found in Finnish Lapland have also been discovered in the other Nordic countries and Russia, which indicates that the trade routes to the north were open from very early times. In the Kemi River Valley, there are vestiges of continuous cereal cultivation from 700 CE, but traces of barley dating back to the Iron Age have also been found. However, it was not until the eleventh century that fixed settlements became established in Finnish Lapland, and from that point on the population began to grow steadily.

The first written references to the Finns and the Saami, who belonged to the same common Uralic proto-race, are to be found in the first century of the present era: there is a clear reference in Tacitus' *Germania*, which was written in 98 CE. Northern Finland is mentioned for the first time in a history of the world written by King Alfred of England. Alfred obtained his information about the north from a letter he received from a Norwegian landowner called Ottar in 892 CE. An Icelandic saga relates that the first ruler of the region was Faravid, who reigned some time around the twelfth century.

The expansion of settlement into Finnish Lapland is indicated by the fact that Kemi was already an important town in the fourteenth century. Another parish in the north at that time was Tornio. King Gustav Vasa of Sweden granted staple rights to the ports of Kemi and Tornio in 1531, which increased the size in the area's population and boosted its economy. The settlement of the north was further encouraged by an order issued by Gustav Vasa in 1550 to populate the wilderness

The King of Sweden awarded staple rights to Tornio in the 1530s, and it rapidly developed into the main centre of trade with Lapland. This drawing by Olaus Magnus made in 1555 illustrates trading in Tornio.

areas of the country, and in the 1590s the parishes of Alatornio and Ylitornio boasted 350 inhabitants. A hundred years later, there were about 700 Finns and 1500 Saamis living in the area comprising present-day Finnish Lapland.

Despite the severe conditions of the region, the northern part of Europe offered good conditions for making a living from fur trapping and fishing. Outsiders, however, saw the place in a different light. The stories they told about Lapland described it as an exotic and strange land. Tales about the mythical north spread largely through a work called *Historia de Gentibus Septentrionalibus* written in 1555 by a Swedish clergyman and cosmopolitan, Olaus Magnus. Magnus based his description partly on stories culled from classical sources, but he also visited the best-known village of the north, Tornio, and the information that he gives is for the most part historically valid. According to him, people living in cold climes were stronger and braver than those who lived in the south. They were also more superstitious:

"They worship the sun, which shines on them the whole summer, offering sacrifices of thanksgiving to it because it has brought light to their darkness and warmth to replace the bitter frosts. For the same reason they worship the moon, because in winter, when the sun is hidden, they constantly avail themselves of its light, except when it is lacking around the time of the new moon. Then, even in daytime, they perform their tasks by the light of the brightest stars, which the shining white snow intensifies by reflecting it. Moreover, these people of the Arctic Circle are led astray by evil spirits into an even more foolish delusion: with fervent prayers and special rites they worship a strip of red cloth fixed to a pole or a spear, believing it to possess some divine power on account of its red colour. Everywhere among the people of the far north there are seers and witches, as if it were their very own country. They are skilful conjurors and can change their own and others' faces into different forms, and by means of these false features they can hide their true demeanour. Nor was it only weapon-bearing men who did this: women and tender maidens, too, could by means of a slight breath of air make their faces at their whim into terrifying, leaden, hairy spectres or embellish them with a treacherous pallor."

In his great work *Atlantica* (1679–1702), Olaus Rudbeck the Elder gives a more mythical picture of Lapland than Olaus Magnus. He claims that in classical times Lapland was already a region that was admired by poets and historians. On the other hand, in many mediaeval works Lapland is described as a culturally impoverished, ugly and remote land of pagans and witches. Some stories even place the abode of the devil in the north and describe the people there as one-eyed cavemen or pygmies. Often the descriptions of Lapland by early travellers are invented or highly exaggerated. One of the early descriptions was written by the French adventurer Louis-Henri Loménie de Brienne, who boasts in his account of his travels that he was the first Frenchman to venture there. His journey took place in the 1650s. After he returned home, de Brienne related in the French court that the people of the north were so ugly that it was impossible even to describe them to such handsome persons as the courtiers. His compatriot, the playwright Jean-François Regnard, who visited Lapland in 1681, for his part brags in his travel journal about how he overthrew the shrines of the Saami and cheated a local shaman out of his drum – when the latter failed to travel to Paris in his trance and bring certain objects back to Regnard. When another Frenchman, Aubry de la

Motraye, visited the Tornio region in the second decade of the eighteenth century, he met an old man who had served as a guide to Regnard's group. According to him, this comfort-loving company had not moved beyond their lodging place; in other words, Regnard's stories were invented or culled from older works.

There were other travellers in Lapland. An Italian priest called Francesco Negri made a journey to Tornio and Inari in the 1660s. Around the same time, Johan Ferdinand Körningh, a Swedish Jesuit priest working in Prague who had sought out missionary work in Lapland, was resident in Tornio. Unlike many other travellers, Körningh describes the women of Lapland in a favourable light: "Some Lapp women have very beautiful features. Their dress is charmingly decorated here and there with tinsel, although their manners are coarse and crude. They place their children in sledges and bind them fast. The child is tossed awkwardly and wretchedly in the sledge when the reindeer runs. It is common for one woman to drive as many as twelve reindeer, and indeed up to twelve sledges, all tied together in a chain. In this way they transport the children." The number of travellers

The reindeer has provided a very important source of livelihood for the inhabitants of Lapland. Reindeer products like meat, hides and antlers have been traded for centuries. In this drawing by Olaus Magnus in 1555 a reindeer is being milked.

continued to grow in the eighteenth century. One of these was an English writer called Matthew Consett, who went there in the 1780s. Consett says of the people of Tornio, that although they lived far from the known world, they were anything but uncivilised. Even the future King of France, the Duc d'Orléans Louis Philippe, visited Lapland in 1795 disguised as a German trader. Gradually, with the work of scientific expeditions, the picture of the inhabitants of the north became more diverse and true-to-life. Admittedly, even in the early nineteenth century, the Swedish religious reformer Lars Levi Laestadius claimed: "Lapland in people's minds is like Scythia to the Greeks, Germania to the Romans and Siberia to the Russians."

INCREASING FINNISH INFLUENCE IN LAPLAND

As a result of pioneer settlement, the population grew faster in Lapland in the seventeenth century than in other parts of Finland. This was particularly so in the interior, beside the rivers and lakes. Elsewhere in the country, the male population was depleted by the succession of wars waged by the Swedish Crown. Moreover, towards the end of the century, Finland suffered the worst years of famine (1695–97) in its history; a third of the country's population died of starvation and disease.

In Lapland the area between the coastal region and the northern Lapp villages had for long been common land used by the Saami and the Finns for hunting and fishing, but now it began to be settled by Finnish pioneers. Some of these had come from the south to escape the heavy tax burdens and the constant conscriptions for military service that were imposed in the era when Sweden was a major European power. The first localities to become Finnish in this sense were Kittilä, Kemijärvi, Muonio, Ranua, Posio, Kuusamo and Sodankylä. In 1642 there were at least three pioneer farms in Kittilä, and by the end of the century Finnish settlement had spread to cover practically the whole parish. Finnish settlement in Kemijärvi began in the 1630s and in Sodankylä in the 1660s. The number of Saamis living in Finnish Lapland at the end of the seventeenth century was about 1500.

The pioneer settlers spread beyond the boundary laid down between Lapland and the farming areas of the north in the fourteenth century. This boundary, which was in fact the northern border of the historical Province of Ostrobothnia, ran from Maanselkä in the Kuusamo region to Kemijärvi, and from there between Sodankylä and Rovaniemi to the Ounas River and on due south along the Kemi River (Map 2, page 35). At first it was illegal to trespass across the border, and the Saamis frequently accused the settlers in local court sessions of destroying their beaver dams and taking their fishing waters. In these disputes, the Swedish Crown took the side of the settlers and opened the border with decrees in 1673 and 1695. It then became possible for those who so desired to establish themselves as settlers in Lapland. The Crown supported the pioneers by awarding them freedom from taxation and exemption from conscription for fifteen years. Trade further developed in Lapland when the Crown founded the city of Oulu in 1605 to be the administrative capital of northern Finland, and soon after that, in 1621, Tornio to be the centre of trade with Lapland.

The collapse of the border between Lapland and the farming regions led to the persecution of the Saamis' religion. The Swedish Crown set out to convert the "wild pagans" with determination, and it did so with considerable violence. Among the best-known of the missionaries was Gabriel Tuderus, the first Rector of Kemi *Lappmark* (an administrative area in Swedish Lapland). He called the Saami "flesh-coveting swine and curs incited by Satan to resist the true, pure and solemn sacraments". Churches began to be built in Lapland as symbols of the Crown's authority. The earliest went up in Inari in 1646, in Kemijärvi in 1647, in Sodankylä (where it still stands as a tourist attraction) in 1689 and in Utsjoki in 1700. Rounala Church in Enontekiö had been built even earlier, in 1607, but it was left on the Swedish side after the new frontier was drawn in 1809.

One of the scourges of the Saami was Olaus Sirma, the Chaplain of Enontekiö. He was himself a Saami born in Sodankylä. He left posterity a very conflicting picture of himself: while he was obviously a talented man, he was ruthless in his suppression of the religious beliefs of his own people, and he was also given to drunkenness. Sirma studied for holy orders at the University of Umeå in Sweden. The well-known Swedish Saami poet Anders Fjellner and Lars Levi Laestadius, the religious reformer, graduated from the same university.

Sirma was also an important informant for the Swedish scholar Johannes Schefferus, whose well-known work *Lapponia* was published in Frankfurt am Main

The wooden church of Sodankylä, built in 1689. The Swedish Crown built the first churches in Lapland in the early 17th century.

The Saami shamans used the drum in their séances. This drawing of a shaman's drum is from Johannes Schefferus' work *Lapponia* (1673).

in 1673. Schefferus never actually visited Lapland himself, basing his information on data supplied to him by priests working in the region. The work was written in Latin, and it came out three years later in French and within ten years in English, German and Dutch, which made it early on the fundamental work of scholarship on Lapland. The book included two Saami-language chants by Sirma. Translated into Latin and French, they were disseminated to become objects of wonder to scholars of the day: "How can such a primitive people living in rudimentary conditions produce poetry of such a high quality?" they marvelled. Later, for example, the famous German poet Johann Gottfried Herder was inspired by the chants and translated them into German. Franz Mikael Franzén, a Finnish poet who was born in Oulu and spent his whole working life in Sweden, where he became a bishop, used one of Sirma's chants in his well-known children's song *Spring, min snälla ren* (Run, My Reindeer, Run).

Finnish Lapland was "possessed" by the outside world in the eighteenth century not only through the travel journals of explorers but also in other ways. The administration of northern Finland was made more effective by the establishment of the Province of Oulu in 1775. And new administrative and ecclesiastical parishes like Sodankylä, Utsjoki, Kemijärvi and Muonio were created in the same century. The objective was to integrate the northern regions more closely with the rest of the realm. At the same time, settlement intensified and spread ever further north, reaching the northernmost parts of Sodankylä. Part of the reason for this was the fact that Finland experienced two violent occupations by Russian forces in the wars of the early part of the century between Sweden and Russia, and some of the population fled north. However, this was not only a period of rising pioneer settlement in Finnish Lapland, but also one of growing trade. There was a flourishing shipbuilding industry in Tornio, and its port was big enough to export the natural riches of Lapland to the markets of Europe.

RELIEF FOR THE PERSECUTED SAAMI

The worst persecution of the Saami religion eased when the people converted, at least ostensibly, to Lutheranism in the eighteenth century. At the same time, the Crown of Sweden also officially approved Finnish as the language of religious

The drum was a tool used by the Saami shamans in their rituals. During his séance, the shaman called on the spirits by beating his drum with a hammer made of reindeer antler until he entered a state of trance. During his trance, the shaman wandered into the realm of the dead, where the departed gave him advice on how to solve particular problems. The marks on the skin of the drum varied according to the region. Originally the patterns were either heliocentric with an image of the sun in the middle, or they the had images depicting the cosmos on three levels: the heavens above, the earth in the middle and the underworld below. The shamans interpreted the marks in these sections in their prophecies.

For modern man, the symbols on the shamans' drums are often extremely difficult to interpret, and moreover the patterns changed in the course of time. Some of them, however, are clear: for example, the drum often had images of a bear, a crane or a wolf or of the God of Thunder or the Antler God. The Saami believed the bear to be the most important of nature's creatures and to be the instrument of the gods. It banished evil spirits and could bring success in hunting. The crane, on the other hand, was thought to be the messenger of the gods, while the wolf had a darker reputation: it was believed to have been created by the devil. The most important of the Saami gods was the Thunder God, who gave man life, protected his health and oversaw his death. The Antler God, for his part, was the god of fertility among both men and animals, and he ruled over the growth of plants.

The Lutheran church regarded shamanism with abhorrence, and the shaman's drum was one of the most persecuted objects. The drums were obliterated so thoroughly from Finnish Lapland that not a single genuine drum has survived there. As late as the 1770s, use of the shaman's drum was punishable by death.

Other objects connected with the worship of "false gods", such as shrines and sacrificial sites, were likewise destroyed. Despite the persecution, a number of shrines have survived in Finnish Lapland, and the sites of numerous shrines have been identified. For example, in Pokka in the municipality of Kittilä, travellers can still see the shrine of Taatsi. The collector of folklore Samuli Paulaharju claimed that the shrine of Taatsi was dedicated to wild reindeer, fish and later to domesticated reindeer. People came from far and wide, even from the mountains of Norway and the lower waters of the Kemi River, to sacrifice there. Sacrifices were brought to the shrine to ensure success in hunting and fishing or to obtain good fortune generally. Most commonly the sacrificers were men. In addition to fish or meat, the offerings often took the form of coins, tobacco or spirits.

In the 16th century, the Swedish Crown implemented a determined campaign to eradicate "paganism" from Lapland. The drums of the Saami shamans were destroyed. On the other hand, a few shrines have been preserved. The picture shows one such shrine in the form of a wooden effigy of a fish. It is located in the rural municipality of Rovaniemi.

There are some early detailed descriptions of Lapland made by scholars. Here an extract of Johannes Schefferus' famous work *Lapponia*, written in 1673.

instruction in the region. The relaxation in relations with the Saami is indicated for instance by the fact that the rights of the nomadic reindeer herders were recognised in the frontier agreement of Strömstad (1751), which has been called the Magna Charta of the Saami. It strictly defined the frontier line between Norway and Sweden: Kautokeino, Karasjok and half of the Parish of Utsjoki were left on the Norwegian side of the border. What was important from the Saamis' point of view was the fact that the document recognised in writing the civic rights of the Saami. Despite the establishment of the new frontier, they were accorded the right to cross it with their reindeer herds into Norway and to return to their winter villages in Finland and Sweden. Each Lapp village (*siida*) followed its traditional routes on its annual migrations. For example, the reindeer of the Rommavuoma village in the parish of Utsjoki first pastured on Pallastunturi and Ounastunturi Fells, then moved into the Muonio area and on to Pajala in Sweden. From there they eventually migrated to the mountains of Norway. The annual nomadic cycle of the village was thus several hundred kilometres long.

One reason for the more relaxed attitude of the authorities was probably the fact that in the eighteenth century the scholarly community in Sweden had tried to make a name for itself in the European scientific world particularly with its research in the north. In the early nineteenth century, too, there were several very sympathetic assessments of Saami culture and traditions, although it was at that time that scientific theories of race began to rise to the fore in Europe. For example, Elias Lönnrot, the famous Finnish collector of folk poetry, toured Finnish Lapland in the 1830s and 1840s. Like the Rector of Utsjoki, Jakob Fellman, he supported the free movement of the Saami over the whole of Lapland. In addition, he thought a "Finnish-Lapp" market town should be established beside the Paats River to boost the Saamis' trade. The Governor of the Province of Oulu likewise followed the development of the living conditions of the Saami of the northern frontier areas in the early nineteenth century with concern. When the Saamis of the Kola Peninsula illegally imposed taxes on the reindeer of the Inari Saamis, the governor personally took the matter to the Governor General in Helsinki and the Governor of the Province of Arkhangelsk.

In the 19th century, the expeditions of travellers from further south in Europe increased with the growth of tourism. Here: *Laplanders*, an etching made by I. R. Cruikshank in 1822 that was exhibited in London.

The thaw in relations with the Saami lasted until the end of the nineteenth century. Then nationalism, an ideology that in Finland took the name "Fennomania", strove to assimilate the people in the north as well. An attitude that was encapsulated in the slogan "One people, one language, one mind" obtained a footing, and this began to be reflected, for example, in the banning of the Saami language in schools. It was not until after the Second World War that the Saami culture and language began once again to receive recognition and support from the state.

EXPLORERS IN LAPLAND

The people of central Europe became aware of Lapland not only from reindeer products and furs but also from the accounts of explorers. French, British, Italian and German travellers provided documented information about conditions in Lapland for the scientific societies and academies that were founded in the eighteenth century. The most significant journey of exploration in Lapland in that century was probably that made in 1736–1737 by Pierre-Louis Moreau de Maupertuis, a member of the Paris Academy of Sciences. The purpose of the exploration was to measure the angle of inclination of the Earth's surface at the Arctic Circle in order to establish whether the orb was flat or curved at its poles. Maupertuis proved that Descartes' curved interpretation was wrong and Newton's flat model correct.

Maupertuis and his team spent nearly a year in Tornio and Ylitornio. Indeed, in the courts of central Europe Tornio became one of the best-known towns in the kingdom of Sweden as a result of the numerous stories that were told about Maupertuis' journey. For example, Voltaire wrote his descriptions of Lapland for a well-known French encyclopaedia on the basis of the travellers' accounts and extolled Maupertius as the "Marquis of the Arctic Circle". As a souvenir of his journey, Maupertius had a portrait painted of himself dressed in a Saami costume against the scenery of the Torne River Valley. The expedition also included some Swedish researchers. The members of the French expedition participated actively in the social life of the small circle of gentry in Tornio. The team returned to Paris bringing with them two Finnish sisters. They were presented to Paris society, but it was reported that they ended up in a convent.

At the end of the century, the road to Tornio was crowded because the travel books had made the town known in Europe. For example, an Englishman called Edward Clarke visited Finnish Lapland in the summer of 1799. He travelled as far as Enontekiö, where he flew in a hot-air balloon in order to study the Saamis, who lived dispersed over the area. The locals immediately gathered to marvel at the balloon, and the Englishman was able to study them. In passing through the Tornio area, Clarke had an opportunity to observe the penal practices of the time:

on twelve poles beside the road hung the hands and bodies of those who had been punished.

The picture of Finnish Lapland given by an Italian called Giuseppe Acerbi, who travelled in Finnish Lapland together with Clarke, is appalling: he claimed, for example, that the inhabitants had odd, unhygienic eating habits. Acerbi and Clarke also frightened the locals by shooting birds for stuffing and putting into collections of curiosities to display to the gentry of Europe. Various exotic plants, Saami costumes, hides and other local objects also ended up in these collections. On the other hand, A. F. Skjöldebrand, a Swede who was a member of Acerbi's group, described the Tornio region as charming and the women as beautiful in his travel account. However, he found the areas further to the north less appealing to the eye.

Young members of the European gentry began to travel to Lapland as part of their education. This practice originated in Britain and became particularly popular in the eighteenth century. The Grand Tour was intended to educate, enlighten and give the finishing touches to these young cosmopolitans. Mostly they went to visit the ancient monuments of Greece and Rome and also to countries in central Europe. Lapland was the Ultima Thule of these journeys.

THE MIDNIGHT SUN

Lapland's first tourist attraction was Aavasaksa Fell beside the Torne River in the parish of Ylitornio. All visitors to Lapland from the seventeenth century on climbed to its peak at Midsummer to view the sun at midnight. Although the peak is only just over 200 metres above sea level, it was regarded as an excellent viewing location. The Frenchman Maupertuis describes Aavasaksa in his travel book in the following way: "It is not easy to reach the summit. First you must walk uphill through forest until you come to a huge rocky open space, after which there is a new stretch of forest which leads to the top. Once there, we had to cut down trees. The north-east side of the fell is frighteningly steep with huge boulders, between which there were a few hawk's nests."

The scenery of Aavasaksa was described in dozens of travel books written by foreigners, and it was also illustrated in landscape drawings by Finns. As a result,

The "nightless" nights of Lapland and the sun which shines at midnight have attracted travellers for centuries. It was thanks to them that Aavasaksa Fell in the municipality of Ylitornio became the first tourist attraction in Finnish Lapland. This drawing of Aavasaksa is from A. F. Skjöldebrands work *Voyage pittoresque au Cap Nord*.

Aavasaksa became perhaps the most famous spot for viewing the midnight sun in Europe. It was described in articles and accounts, and its scenery even became familiar to readers as a setting in the plots of novels like the Swedish writer Frederika Bremer's story of personal intrigue *Midsommar-resan*, written in 1848. In his work *Finland framstäldt i teckningar* (1845–52), the celebrated Finnish writer Zacharias Topelius described how around midsummer Tornio was swarming with travellers on their way to Aavasaksa.

It was sun worship than made Aavasaksa famous. In all the kingdoms of Europe, the sun and the sun god Apollo symbolised the splendour and the secular and divine power of the ruler. In the seventeenth century, the so-called "nightless night" of Lapland was even considered a proof that Sweden was the mythical Atlantis, the cradle of all civilisation. In 1695, Swedish scientists made an astronomic expedition to the Tornio region to observe the movements of the sun. Preparations for the expedition had begun the previous year after Gustav XI of Sweden visited Tornio to view the midnight sun. In honour of his visit, a bas relief was made with the inscription "To the unsetting sun another benign Sun". The English writer and traveller Bayard Taylor, who visited the Torne Valley area in 1857, states in his book *Northern Travel*: "Nothing in Italy, nothing in the Tropics, equals the magnificence of the Polar skies." The popularity of Aavasaksa as a tourist destination continued to grow in the 1870s, when the Finnish government bought up large areas of the region for tourism.

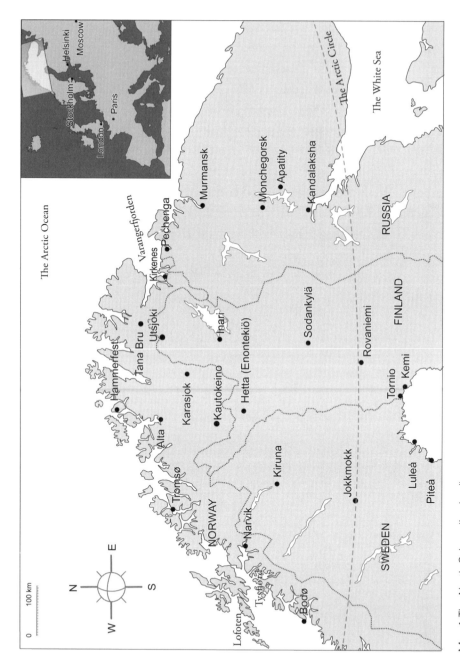

Map 1. The North Calotte (Lapland)

One person who helped to make conditions in Lapland better known was the natural scientist Carl von Linné (before his ennoblement: Linnaeus), who became the most internationally celebrated Swedish scientist of the eighteenth century. His journey to Lapland in 1732, the collection of flowers that he made there and *Flora Lapponica,* the book that he made of the collection, increased the world's awareness of conditions in the northern parts of Europe. Linné had been encouraged to go to Lapland by his teacher, Olaus Rudbeck the Younger, who had been there himself in 1695.

Immediately after his expedition to Lapland, Linné made an educational journey to Holland, Britain and France. He took with him a Saami costume and the notes of his expedition to Lapland. In Holland he, too, had a portrait painted of himself wearing a Saami costume. The costume was a proof that a person had really been in Lapland, while the portrait represented the tourist snapshot of the day. A Saami costume had been displayed in the French royal court in the seventeenth century, and some exotic animals classified as reindeer had been shipped to the same destination as early as the fifteenth century.

Linné's journey in Lapland took him from Tornio up along the Swedish bank of the Torne River as far as Junosuando. On his way back from Lapland, Linné travelled down the west coast of Finland to Turku,

The cover of Linnaeus' *Flora Lapponica.*

from where he returned to Sweden by ship. In his travel account, he describes the nature of Lapland as clean. According to him, the people there still lived in a blissful natural state. He instructed the visitor to Lapland to read the signs of nature: the branches of big pines were dense on the south side, while on the north side there were few branches; on the south side of anthills grew hay, blueberries and lingonberries, but on the north side nothing; the bark of aspen trees was smooth on the south side, rough on the north. He advised: "The Saami are able to travel in the pathless forests using these signs; you do likewise."

2

THE BIRTH OF FINNISH LAPLAND

PLAGUES AND FAMINES

In the early nineteenth century, a war broke out between Sweden and Russia as a result of which Finland's 700-year-old bond with Sweden was severed, and it became an autonomous Grand Duchy within the Russian Empire. The Finnish War was only a small northern episode in the series of confrontations called the Napoleonic Wars that convulsed Europe, but it was an important event in the history of Finland. The war began on 21 February 1808, when Russian forces invaded south-east Finland. They rapidly advanced over the frontier in three directions. The main force pushed forward along the coast, and by March it had occupied Helsinki and Turku, the country's major cities. Another army advanced through central Finland towards Ostrobothnia, while a third marched on Tornio. Altogether twelve field battles were waged on Finnish soil between April and October 1808, the fiercest of them in the area of Ostrobothnia in western Finland.

The Swedish-Finnish forces withdrew before the Russian advance to Tornio in November 1808. Although no further battles were fought in this area, the billeting

One song has described Lake Inari as so deep that nobody has measured it. For the local inhabitants, the lake has been, and still is, important for fishing and leisure activities.

of thousands of badly wounded, exhausted and starving soldiers in the small villages of the Alatornio region was disastrous. The soldiers were crammed into cabins and farmsteads together with their inhabitants. An epidemic rapidly spread through the area, killing thousands of soldiers and locals. The Chief Physician of the Swedish-Finnish army stated in his report to the King: "The disease has developed from cattarhal inflammation into septic fever, which contaminates the air and produces a dangerous and fatal contagion."

It is estimated that over a period of three months, from December 1808 to February 1809, over 2000 soldiers died. The mortality figures for the Parish of Alatornio also multiplied: in 1809 the number of deaths in the parish was about 620 when it was normally around 150. The mortality of the population in Lapland during the Finnish War was the worst in the whole century, unsurpassed even by the death figures for the harsh famine years of the 1860s.

This happened because of the Swedish army's failure to supply adequate food and medication. And the location of sick soldiers in cramped and unhygienic conditions only exacerbated the situation. There was very little food available, and this lowered people's resistance. Practically the only medicine that was used was liquor, there were few doctors, and some of them died of the same diseases as their patients. What was called "field disease" in fact covered several different contagions, such as dysentery, typhoid and nervous fever.

The epidemics during the Finnish War mainly affected the coastal parishes, but there was a fever epidemic in the interior of Lapland as well. There, however, people had other, more pressing concerns. Living conditions had deteriorated with the succession of crop failures that began in 1807. They continued up till 1813, and these years are known in the folk tradition as the seven years of famine. During this time, people in the parishes of the interior literally starved to death. Sodankylä and Kemijärvi were the worst hit areas; the crop failures naturally affected those parts when agriculture had gained a foothold. On the other hand, those inhabitants of Lapland who lived by fishing, hunting and reindeer herding were spared the worst. But the situation for them too deteriorated because game and fish were also in short supply in those years. The crop failure was so severe in 1810 that it exceeded any in living memory. The situation is indicated by the fact that the fields and meadows

The epidemics that broke out during the Finnish War (1808–09) particularly affected the inhabitants of the Alatornio region. The Finnish national poet J. L. Runeberg's classic work *The Tales of Ensign Stål* contains this picture of a wounded Finnish soldier drawn by the great Finnish artist Albert Edelfelt.

were still covered with snow in July. People resorted to eating roots, sorrel and the flesh of animals that had starved to death. Some left and took to begging in order to survive, while many just fell by the road and died of the cold. Some fled to the White Sea coast in Russia, and some to northern Norway, where they could earn a living by fishing. This was the first of the waves of emigration in the nineteenth century.

Tornio Orthodox Church. When Finland came under Russian domination in 1809, a Russian barracks was built in Tornio, and in conjunction with it a Russian Orthodox congregation was established.

FINNISH LAPLAND

The Finnish War was an important turning point in the history of Lapland. The war ended with the signing of the Peace Treaty of Hamina on 17 September 1809, and the surrender of territory by Sweden that the treaty provided for created the concept of "Finnish Lapland". The area of Swedish Lapland that was surrendered comprised the *Lappmarks* of Kemi and Torne (Tornio). The annexed territory was made into the Jurisdictional District of Tornio, which was part of the Province of Oulu (see Map 2). Later the jurisdictional district was split into two so that the northernmost parts (Muonio, Kolari, Enontekiö, Kittilä, Sodankylä, Inari and Utsjoki) formed the Jurisdictional District of Lapland (1837), while the parishes along the Torne River, including Tornio itself, were attached to the Jurisdictional

Map 2.
The territory
annexed
to Finland
in 1809

☐ Tornio Jurisdictional District: The territory annexed to Finland in 1809

⊟ The border between Lapland and Finland in the 17th century

District of Kemi. In time (1938), these two jurisdictional districts came to comprise the Province of Lapland.

As a result of Finland becoming part of the Russian Empire, a small Russian garrison was stationed in Tornio. There were between thirty and seventy Cossacks belonging to the 24th Don Regiment stationed there over the years together with their officers and an Orthodox priest who led the Russian congregation. Legend has it that the men of Tornio were jealous of their women, who seemed to enjoy the company of the handsome Cossacks. Indeed there were a number of Russian-Finnish marriages, and a few Finnish wives moved with their husbands to Russia when their three-year period of service in Tornio ended. The total number of Russian troops stationed in Finland varied from 55,000 at the beginning of the nineteenth century to 9000 at the end of it.

In 1846 Jakov Grot, a Russian official stationed by the Tsar in Helsinki, visited the Tornio region in the company of his friend, the great Finnish collector of folk poetry Elias Lönnrot. Grot's first impression of Lapland was favourable. In his travel journal, he praises the people of the north for being more hospitable than southerners. They were also, according to him, unselfish and honest. Grot travelled only as far as Aavasaksa. Difficult travel conditions made descriptions of central and northern Lapland much less common than those of the area along the Torne River, where most of the travellers headed.

Certainly there are some descriptions of the more northern areas too, written by clergymen. For example, the Rector of Enontekiö Erik Grape described conditions there at the turn of the eighteenth and nineteenth centuries. The parish of Enontekiö was more dramatically affected by the new frontier in 1809 than any other parish in Lapland. The border cut the parish in half. The old church was felt to be too near to the border, and it was moved further away to the village of Hetta. The new border, which followed the Könkämä River, also meant that some of the Saami population of the village remained on the Swedish side of the border, and with intensive settlement by pioneers, Finnish influence in the parish began to increase rapidly. It has been calculated that 67% of the population of Enontekiö were Saamis in 1810, but by 1900 their number had fallen to 10%. The drastic nature of the change is also partly due to the fact that some of the Saamis who moved into

C. G. Gillberg's copper print depicting an inhabitant of the Parish of Tornio in 1890.

the parish as settlers were officially registered as Finns. Grape describes the Saamis and the Finns as being rather similar. Their habitations were equally primitive whether they were the tepee-like *kotas* of the Saami or the chimneyless cabins of the settlers. The standard of living and level of education of the two groups were also about the same.

Jakob Fellman, the Rector of Utsjoki and Inari described the living conditions of his own Saami congregation in favourable terms. Although the natural conditions of the region were miserable and travel connections weak, the people of Utsjoki were well aware of their rights. They demanded to have annual local court sessions, church services and baptisms in their own parish. When these were not arranged, they sent a letter of complaint to the Governor of the Province of Oulu, and the minister acted as their emissary. According to Fellman, among the Saami of the area, most of whose family roots lay in Norway, the nomadic reindeer herders constituted the upper social stratum. On the other hand, Fellman thought that when it came to religious devotion the reindeer herders were far behind the Saamis who lived by fishing.

In Utsjoki too, a hundred years later, the collector of folklore Samuli Paulaharju admired the rich reindeer-herding nomads who travelled over the fells like princes in their colourful Saami costumes. The ordinary fishing Saamis gaped at their striking passage with wonder. At the lowest rank among the Saamis were the reindeer-herding hands who worked for Finns. All in all, the society of the Saami was just as hierarchical as that of the Finns.

However, not all the Finns agreed with the favourable picture of the northern regions drawn by the priests. For example, the Finnish scholar Mathias Alexander Castrén who was the first professor of the Finnish language, travelled to central and northern Lapland in 1838, and he offers a much gloomier description of the area. According to him, once a traveller passed beyond the Arctic Circle, he entered the realm of frozen darkness, and few were the glimmers of light that awaited him there. Castrén was born in Tervola, south of Rovaniemi, and he had lived in the

Among the latest tourist attractions in Lapland are canoeing safaris, white-water rafting and mountaineering. At Korouoma in Posio one can do ice climbing.

north since the age of twelve. His account gives a good description of just how much, even in the nineteenth century, the remote roadless parishes beyond the Arctic Circle differed from the region around the lower waters of the Kemi River. The road from Rovaniemi to Sodankylä was not completed until 1902, that to Inari in 1925 and that to Utsjoki in 1957. The Rector of Utsjoki, Anders Andelin, stated with a sigh when he eventually arrived exhausted at his post: "Travel in Lapland is laborious be it winter or summer!"

THE NORTHERN DIMENSION OF THE CRIMEAN WAR

The Crimean War, which convulsed Europe, also affected Finland and its northern regions. Anglo-French forces captured and destroyed 120 Finnish ships in all, and they also burnt shipyards and vessels in nearly all the Finnish ports on the Gulf of Bothnia. In early June 1854, the people of Tornio feared that the enemy would attack their town, too, as two other northern towns, Oulu and Raahe, had already been visited by the enemy. So they packed their chattels and fled. British officers landed in Tornio on 8 June 1854. They talked to the mayor and inspected the warehouses, after which they left without burning anything. It was a different story in other ports, where the actions of the British left strong anti-British sentiments smouldering among the coastal Finns.

The bitter memories of the Crimean War were surprisingly revived in March 1857, when the British newspapers *The Times* and the *Daily News* showed pictures of the miserable conditions in the Finnish countryside. It was a year of severe crop failure, and the pictures well reflected this. The accompanying articles related that people's plight was so great that the poor children were eating their own fingers! They reported that it was particularly the people of the ports burnt by the British in the Crimean War that were suffering.

A group of British businessmen decided to organise a public collection to aid the needy in the Finnish coastal towns. The hostile attitude to the British in Finland was having unfortunate consequences for trade, and they wished to correct this. Thus two businessmen from Leeds, Joseph Sturge and Thomas Harvey, travelled to Finland, and they were followed by another pair, George Barker and Wilson Sturge, who visited Tornio in 1857. The aid was addressed expressly to the inhabitants of northern Finland to compensate them for the destruction of their boats and nets during the war.

Dozens of British businessmen participated in the collection, and over £7000 was amassed for distribution to those in need. Aid was also given by the Russian nobility and business associates in Saint Petersburg. There were likewise some donations from collections made in Sweden and from German cities like Lübeck and Hamburg. In Finland, too, aid was collected in churches for those who had been made destitute by the crop failures in the north. One consequence of these collections was the fact that Lapland and the northern regions became better known both in Europe generally and in other parts of Finland.

THE *FELLESDISTRIKT*

The nineteenth century was an era of frontier closures. During it, the borders of Finnish Lapland became more strictly defined on paper and more accurately demarcated on the ground. The frontier drawn between Sweden and Finland/ Russia was drawn along the Torne and Muonio Rivers. This provoked Russia and

The main village of Muonio seen from the church tower. The landscape in Muonio is dominated by the Muonio River, which, running as it does along the national frontier, has been one of the most important passages between Tornio and northern Norway.

Norway to define more strictly a jointly administered common frontier region in the north called the *Fellesdistrikt*.

This common region in the North Calotte (approximately equivalent to the area known in English as Lapland) that was jointly administered by Russia (and earlier also Novgorod), Norway and Sweden had a long history. At its most extensive, in the thirteenth century, the area covered the Kola Peninsula, Finnish Lapland and the Arctic Ocean border as far as Lyngen in Norway. In the seventeenth century, there was a dispute between Norway (which was then ruled by Denmark) and Sweden over the area. Sweden lost, and in 1613 it was excluded from access to the Arctic Ocean. The borders of the region were again re-defined in 1751, when the frontier between Norway and Sweden was drawn up more exactly. Discussions about what remained of the common area were conducted between Russia and the then allied kingdoms of Sweden and Norway in 1825 and 1826. As Finland was not an independent state, it was not invited to the negotiating table and was obliged to look on as the Sør Varanger area was divided up. The same thing happened again in 1852, when Norway and Russia decided to close their borders to the nomadic reindeer herders (who had previously been allowed to cross them freely as they followed their herds) and also to fishermen. Access to the Arctic coast, where large sections of the population of northern Finland travelled to fish every year, was thus cut off, and many Finns had to take Norwegian nationality in order to be able to continue their fishing activities. The last border to be closed to the reindeer herders was that between Finland and Sweden in 1889.

The people of Finnish Lapland had originally feared that the consequences of the frontier closures would be only unfavourable. This turned out not to be true, however. When the large herds of the Norwegian and Swedish Saamis were no longer able to graze on the Finnish fells, new pastures became available to the reindeer herders of Inari and Enontekiö, and the reindeer stocks in these parishes grew considerably in the latter half of the nineteenth century.

LAESTADIANISM

In the nineteenth century, the life of the Saamis, Finns, Norwegians and Swedes throughout the North Calotte region was convulsed by a powerful religious

Saami-language literature

The first writing in one of the Saami languages in the North Calotte has been dated to 1557, when an English sea captain called Stephen Borrough compiled a list of 95 words and expressions used in the Saami language spoken in northern Russia. Otherwise, it was mainly the local clergy who compiled and recorded writing in the Saami languages. In northern Sweden, the Rector of Piteå, Nicolaus Andreae Rhen, published the first Saami-language alphabet primer in 1619. Another minister, Johannes Tornaeus, published his *Manuale Lapponicum* partly in North Saami in 1648, while Pastor Petrus Fjällström published the Old Catechism in South Saami as well as a grammar and Swedish-Saami dictionary in 1738. The religious reformer Lars Levi Laestadius also published a religious tract in Lule Saami in the early eighteenth century.

In Finnish Lapland too, some texts have been preserved, albeit much fewer. Johannes Schefferus' *Lapponia (1673)* contains two poems written in the dialect of Kemi *Lappmark*. In the eighteenth century, the view became prevalent in the church that the word of God must be preached to the people in their own language so that they might be persuaded to adopt the Lutheran faith. Therefore, the ministers who worked in Lapland were required to possess a knowledge of the local Saami language. This applied particularly to the parishes of Utsjoki, Enontekiö and Inari. Some clergymen refused to accept this. For example, Henrik Wegelius, who was Rector of Utsjoki in the eighteenth century, called Saami "a cur's language". On the other hand, by the advent of the Age of Romanticism in the nineteenth century, the attitude of the local clergy to the study of Saami had warmed somewhat. For example, the Rector of Utsjoki Jakob Fellman studied Saami and wrote religious works in it. A later rector of the same parish, F. W. Stierncreutz, also studied Saami and took a public examination in the language before his parishioners in 1851.

Mostly the "literature" of the Saami even in the nineteenth century was oral: legends and chants that were handed down from one generation to the next. The pioneer in written narrative was a Swedish Saami called Johan Turi, who published a book entitled *Muitalus sámiid birra* in 1910. This was translated and published in English as *Turi's Book of Lapland* in 1931. It describes in lively detail the everyday life and the festivities of the Saami. According to Turi, he wished to record everything about the way of life and the conditions of the Saami so that there would be no need to ask about the Saamis' situation, and no need to distort it. One early work written by a non-Saami describing the life of the Saami that deserves mention is *Om Lappland och Lapparne* (On Lapland and the Lapps); it was written by a Swede called Gustav von Düben in 1873, and it gives an extensive account of the life, customs and culture of this northern people.

revivalist movement, which in fact became the first popular mass movement of the people of the north. The movement began to be called Laestadianism after its leader Lars Levi Laestadius (1800–1861), the Rector of Karesuando and Pajala in Sweden. Laestadius' father was a penniless pioneer farmer from Arjeplog in Swedish Lapland, one of whose ancestors had come to Lapland as a minister in the seventeenth century. Laestadius' mother, on the other hand, was a Saami. The birth of early Laestadianism has been dated to 1846, when Laestadius began to deliver the sermons which later became so famous. Laestadius himself named a Saami woman, Milla Clementsdotter (known as "Mary of Lapland"), whom he had met two years previously, as his spiritual inspiration in creating the new movement. Behind his conversion there were also some personal tribulations: the death of his child and his own ill health. Laestadius' aim was to purge his parishioners of lip-serving Christianity, drinking and immorality. Despite its criticism of the official Lutheran church, the movement remained within its bosom.

The authorities in the nineteenth century regarded Laestadianism with suspicion. During religious services, the members of the congregation were given to noisy movements, leaping and shouting with joy and publicly confessing their sins. For this, dozens of women were fined in local courts for disturbance of the peace in church; most of the congregation thus transported were women, although the leaders of the movement were exclusively men, and only men were allowed to preach.

In their sermons Laestadius and his followers used the popular vernacular, which was not lacking in oaths. One of the authorities of that time states in his travel report that a civilised person definitely could not bear to listen to the services of the Laestadians because expressions that offended his sense of decency were used in them. According to Laestadius, this frank language was necessary if the sinful people were to be able to look into their inner world and experience the true faith.

Laestadius was also known in his own time elsewhere in Europe, at least in France. In 1838, he was host to the French scientists Paul Gaimard and Xavier Marmier during their journey from Alta in northern Norway to Tornio. Laestadius had travelled with them all the way from Norway, and during the journey he had regaled his fascinated companions with stories of Saami witches. The three also had common scientific interests. Laestadius gave the French scholars not only

Rector Petrus Laestadius preaching to the Saami in 1828, with some French travellers looking on. This picture was originally published in Daniel von Hogguér's travel book *Reise nach Lappland* (1841).

information about the climatic observations that he had recorded over many years but also a collection of wild plants comprising thousands of specimens. For this, he was made a Chevalier of the Légion d'Honneur in 1841.

In the following year (1839), Marmier paid another visit to Laestadius' cabin. This time he was accompanied one Mme Léonie d'Aunet, whose husband was recording the expedition in his sketches. The lady was not favourably impressed by the preacher. According to her, he was rude, arrogant and boorish. He spoke to people uncouthly with his hat on and his pipe in his mouth and "imagined himself to be someone of importance". To top it all, this "grouch" served them only barley pies, fish and turnips and charged them for it into the bargain.

In Finnish Lapland, Laestadianism attracted followers initially in the parishes along the border with Sweden (Ylitornio, Kolari, Muonio and Enontekiö) and in Kittilä. In the second half of the nineteenth century, the movement spread to other parts of Finnish Lapland, to southern Finland and along with emigration to America and Russia. Northern Norway was also a strong Laestadian area. At the end of the nineteenth century Laestadianism split into five different sects.

THE ROAD TO SCHOOL

Right up to the nineteenth century, responsibility for teaching children in Finland lay mainly with the parents, whose execution of this duty was supervised by the parish priests. To support the parents, the church began to establish so-called "catechetical schools" in Lapland. They were mainly intended for the Saami population, but the system was also used in those parishes with large Finnish populations where there were no parish schools.

The first school teachers in Lapland had been the missionaries sent out by the Lutheran church, who had toured round the region from the seventeenth century on. However, in 1723 the King of Sweden issued a decree on the teaching of Christianity to the Saami and the establishment of schools for young children. The first parish in Finnish Lapland to get its own missionary school was Utsjoki in 1728, but it ceased operating in 1750 when the educational system was reformed, and the Utsjoki school became a catechetical school. Enontekiö received a similar institution in 1780 and Sodankylä in 1781. Altogether about forty persons worked as catechist teachers in these schools in Finnish Lapland in the nineteenth century. Some of them worked in their own native parishes. The children received instruction for at most three months of the year, so the system was not particularly effective. The catechist toured round the hamlets teaching the children. The lessons were sometimes held in the smoky cabins, sometimes in the open air. Thus the teaching also reached those children who did not live in the villages where there were churches.

The educational system was reformed again at the end of the nineteenth century,

In the 19th century, the literacy of the people of Finnish Lapland was estimated to be just as high as that of the rest of the population of Finland. Saamis from Sodankylä learning to read in 1928.

and the catechists were trained into professional peripatetic teachers whose remit was similar to that of the catechists. The reason for the reform was that the first Elementary School Decree had been passed in Finland in 1866, and as a result elementary schools began to be built. The circuit schools operated in Lapland right up to the 1930s. Despite their nature, it was possible to attain an adequate education in these schools: an episcopal visitation in the nineteenth century reported that the children of Lapland could read, write and do arithmetic just as well as the children of the common people in southern Finland. Thus the comments that occasionally appeared in travellers' accounts that the educational level of the people of Finnish Lapland was lower than in the rest of the country were unfounded.

The settler communities of Karabella

Because agriculture in the nineteenth century was still so primitive, successive years of crop failure particularly affected the people of Finnish Lapland who had taken up cattle farming. They then moved to northern Norway, where a few individual Finnish families had already moved in the seventeenth century. In the war years of the eighteenth century, they went there in larger numbers to take up fishing or farming, and at this point, if not earlier, they began to be called Kvens. Migration intensified as a consequence of the crop failures that afflicted Finnish Lapland in particular. These happened in the second decade of the nineteenth century, in the 1830s and again in the 1860s. The peak of migration to northern Norway was in the 1860s and 1870s. The main centres of Finnish settlement were Skibotn and Alta in the area around Lyngen Fjord and the Vardö region in eastern Finnmark. In 1890 there were about 7000 Finnish settlers living in northern Norway. Finns had also settled in northern Sweden at an early stage, and Finnish was, and still is, spoken

The town of Tornio celebrated its third centenary in 1921. The celebrations were officially opened with a drum battery.

throughout the area along the Torne River Valley. Today the language differs from standard Finnish, and it is called *meän kieli* (our language).

Some Finns also emigrated in the nineteenth century to the Arctic Ocean coast of the Kola Peninsula in Russia. Numerous small communities of settlers who had come from northern Norway or Finnish Lapland grew up there. The area later came to be called Petsamo in Finnish (Russian: Pechenga), and it belonged to Finland from 1920 to 1944. In the nineteenth century the area was not permanently settled, but groups of Saami or Russian fishermen regularly travelled through it. It came under Russian control early on, as is evidenced by the fact that the Monastery of Pechenga was built in the 1530s. In 1860 the Tsar permitted foreigners to settle in the region on the condition that they took Russian nationality. A government policy supporting pioneer settlement that was adopted eight years later further intensified immigration to the area.

The Finns founded their first colony on the coast of the Kola Peninsula at Ura in 1864, while the Norwegians established themselves in Vaitolakhti, Zemlyanskaya and beside the Pechenga Fjord. The name Karabella comes from the bay between the Rybachy Peninsula and the mainland, and settlements spread along each side of it. In 1867 there were altogether 114 Finns and 61 Norwegians living in the area. The Russian authorities praised the Finnish settlers who were interested in agriculture as being "the best element" among the settlers of the Arctic coast. By the 1880s there were about 630 Finns living in eleven villages there. The largest villages were Pumangi and Ura. The main livelihood of the settlers was fishing, but every family also kept a few cows and sheep and tilled some small fields around their cabins. The main problem for the settlers was the absence of any Lutheran minister or schools. Some of the coastal Finns crossed over to Finnish Lapland to have any necessary ecclesiastical matters dealt with. There were also itinerant Finnish ministers who performed burial rites, marriages and baptisms and examined children for their knowledge of the catechism and literacy.

In 1899 Finns still composed about 42% of the population of the Russian Arctic coast. After that Russian migration to the area increased, and some of the Finns emigrated from there to America. When the Second World War broke out, most of the population was removed to other parts of the Soviet Union.

3

THE LAND OF SAAMIS
AND SETTLERS

THE SPREAD OF REINDEER HUSBANDRY

Although traces of the practice of herding domesticated reindeer have been found in Siberia dating from the second century BCE and in Norway from the eighth century CE, pastoral reindeer husbandry did not become a common phenomenon until the seventeenth century, and it came to Finnish Lapland even later than that. It has been conjectured that the shift over to nomadic reindeer herding with its concomitant annual seasonal migrations caused the stocks of wild reindeer to decrease.

In Finnish Lapland, large-scale reindeer husbandry was practised in the Enontekiö region from the eighteenth century on; it was not adopted elsewhere there until the following century. However, most of the inhabitants, both Saamis and settlers, owned small numbers of reindeer, which were used as draught animals to transport people and goods and for slaughter to provide food and raw materials for other products. Reindeer products were the nomads' most important barter

The globeflower *(Trollius europaeus)* is an impressive plant. In Lapland it grows wild in meadows and beside brooks. It is the official flower of the Province of Lapland.

goods. The reindeer's hides, antlers and the glue that was produced when the antlers were boiled down, as well as the meat, blood, hoofs, clothes and other artefacts made from their hides and bones were in high demand. In return for these goods, the people of the north obtained flour, butter and liquor.

When Finland's frontiers were closed and the passage of reindeer from Norway, Russia and Sweden was obstructed in the nineteenth century, the pastures that had previously been used by Norwegian and Swedish herders became available to their

Hunting has always been an important source of livelihood for the people of Lapland. This picture from 1925 shows a Saami man with a bear he has killed.

The reindeer-herding nomads used the *kota*, an easily assembled tepee-like dwelling, as they followed their herds to their summer, autumn, winter and spring grazing ranges. This picture was taken in 1925.

Villagers from Palojärvi in Enontekiö setting out to cut hay. The harvesting of hay from natural meadows constituted an import part of agricultural work in Finnish Lapland.

Finnish counterparts. This led to a growth in the size of Finnish reindeer stocks. It has been estimated that in 1800 there were altogether 4000 head of reindeer in Inari, 90% of which were owned by Saamis. By 1900 the number had increased to 34,600, with 92% of them Saami-owned. Indeed, at the end of the nineteenth century, Inari became the parish with the highest reindeer population in Finnish Lapland: on average there were 25 reindeer to every inhabitant. Utsjoki had about 5400 reindeer in 1900, about half of which were owned by just two families; the ownership of the reindeer had shifted in the mid-eighteenth century to an ever-decreasing number of families. In same year Enontekiö had a reindeer population of about 8300, which meant that on average each member of the parish owned nine animals.

Reindeer husbandry was based on an annual cycle. Early in the year, before calving, the reindeer roamed free. After calving, they were rounded up, separated and the calves were marked by cutting the owners' marks in their ears with a sharp knife. The mark indicated the village, clan and individual that the animal belonged to. The animals designated for slaughter were also separated out. The separations could last several weeks, and they traditionally constituted an important form of social intercourse. The calves might also be earmarked in the autumn, when the herds were counted. The reindeer were only tended at certain times of the year. In the 1960s, the use of snowmobiles became common, which facilitated rounding-up. Today snow-crawlers and helicopters are also used. Reindeer husbandry has also changed in many other respects: for example, winter feeding of the reindeer is now practised much more than it used to be. Also, reindeer husbandry has become merely a subsidiary livelihood for the majority of the reindeer herders of Finnish Lapland.

Women have played a central role in reindeer-herding families, taking part in practically all the tasks involved in reindeer husbandry. It is known from the early twentieth century that girls began tending the reindeer when they were still young, about ten years of age. After a couple of years, they were expected to be capable of guarding the gravid

The costumes of the Saamis of Finnish Lapland varied according to where they lived. This picture, which originally appeared in T. I. Itkonen's book *Suomen Lappalaiset* (The Lapps of Finland) in 1948, shows a woman's headdress from the Utsjoki region. It has Norwegian influences and dates from the 1870s.

cows, and soon they had to take responsibility for the herding. Samuli Paulaharju wrote: "With a lasso wound round her shoulders, her own dog at her heels, a girl follows the herds over the wilds, calling orders to her dog and chanting to scare off the wolves howling on the fells." In August, in addition to their herding duties the girls collected hay, which was used to line the traditional reindeer hide boots instead of socks. The hay was first softened by beating it with a spiked board or by thrashing it against a rock and then dried. The womenfolk also collected lichen and hay as fodder and participated in fishing trips both on the rivers and lakes and on the Arctic Ocean. In the evening, it was the duty of the women and girls to make clothes and ropes, look after the children and do the housework. The Swedish Saami writer Johan Turi relates in a famous work "Turi's Book of Lapland" that when she was herding a Saami woman was obliged to give birth in the open air: "There was nothing for that woman to do but to tuck it into the front of her tunic and go on driving the herd till she reached the place where the tents were to be put up." In 1898, the Finnish government introduced a system of reindeer herding cooperatives in Lapland. This meant increased state control over reindeer husbandry. For example, the state could regulate how many reindeer each reindeer herding cooperative was allowed to have. There are today several dozen reindeer herding cooperatives in Finnish Lapland, and at the end of the twentieth century there were about 200,000 reindeer in the province.

THE DAILY LIFE OF THE SETTLERS

The other element of the population of Finnish Lapland, the pioneers settlers, went there with high hopes. There was game aplenty, the waters were brimming with fish, and they had been exempted from military service and from taxes for a stipulated period. The Crown also gave them a patch of land to clear and till. The worst drawback in the settlers' otherwise blissful existence was the harsh climate and environment.

During his short lifespan, the daily life of the nineteenth-century settler consisted of work from dawn till dusk. The pioneer settler undertook to turn the patch of land he received into a farm, and he was obliged to report to the authorities on his progress every year. In the first year, he would generally build a sauna and a

A pioneer settler's farm on the shore of Lake Keimiöjärvi in Muonio. Lapland began to be settled by pioneers on a regular basis from the 17th century on In the 19th century, hundreds of settler farms were established even north of the Arctic Circle.

cabin, which usually consisted of a large living room with one or two recesses. Most of the cabins in the nineteenth century had no chimneys. In the following year it was the turn of the cowshed, and then came the outbuildings. The buildings usually formed an enclosed yard, with only the sauna outside at some distance from the other structures because it constituted a fire risk. The farm was usually located beside a lake or river, and along with the other inhabitants of the village the pioneer farmer enjoyed usufruct of the fishing grounds and the surrounding forest. In addition to putting up the buildings, the farmer was obliged to clear and drain the land, to fence it off (against animal predators) and to harvest hay from the natural meadows. In summer the family would prepare to set off on trips lasting

Peräntie Farm in Alatornio. The largest farms in Finnish Lapland are situated in the Torne River Valley.

National costumes became fashionable in Finland in the 1880s along with the rise of the nationalist movement and the burgeoning enthusiasm for local culture. The models for them were taken from old folk costumes. The national costume of Peräpohjola (southern Lapland) shown here is one of the oldest in the country (1922).

several days to harvest the hay in the outlying fields. The older folk and small children stayed at home to tend the few cows and sheep that the family possessed.

The life of settler families in the nineteenth century was overshadowed not only by repeated years of crop failure but also by a high infant mortality rate. The most general causes of death among babies were smallpox, measles, whooping cough and diphtheria. Mothers also frequently died in childbirth. Another fearsome disease that took its toll of the adult population was tuberculosis. In those days, an accident usually meant death, for the injuries and wounds caused by attacks from wild animals, falling or being crushed by a falling tree had to be treated at home in unhygienic conditions. If the victim did not bleed to death, he died from his wounds becoming infected.

Contagious diseases were another scourge. The antidotes were strong liquor and natural products, whose applications were handed down as lore. A person who had fallen ill to a highly contagious disease might be isolated and left alone to die, but generally the sick were treated at home, which increased the risk of contagion. Saami families had used amulets and spells to ward off diseases for a long time, but the Finnish settlers of Lapland also had their own charms and spells. People

Saamis on the stages of Europe

The practice of taking members of exotic racial minorities and putting them on show in the circuses and music halls of the big cities of Europe had its roots in the "souvenirs" brought back by explorers from their travels and in the early Romantic concept of "the noble savage". In the eighteenth century, Tahitians, Inuits, native Americans and others were put on display, and along with them there were Saamis from Lapland, who caused a sensation among the public and earned money for the impresarios. These exhibitions of indigenous peoples were most common in the nineteenth century. Most of the Saamis who were thus exhibited were from Sweden or Norway. In the first half of the nineteenth century, it was mainly freaks that were put on show: for example, a Saami man who was less than a metre tall and a Saami girl who was 190 cm in height.

A small Saami family that was sent with some reindeer from Stavanger in Norway to London also attained some celebrity. In 1822 the family entertained audiences in a music hall by singing, dancing and playing the violin. The stage backdrop was a painting depicting Nordkap. The show achieved a phenomenal popularity, and over a couple of months the Saamis attracted 58,000 spectators.

At the end of the nineteenth century, the nature of the exhibitions changed: the focus shifted from exhibitions of freaks to a scientific interest in the whole Saami people and its culture. The Anthropological Society of Berlin exhibited a family from Karesuando in 1875, and at the same time another Saami family with their reindeer, dogs, skis and household objects was brought to the city. A group including ten or so Saamis and reindeer were shipped from northern Norway by way of Turku to Paris in 1878. They were the subject of an extensive exhibition that also presented their jewellery, buckles, knives and bags.

The fascination of the French for Lapland is illustrated by the fact that the anthropologist Prince Ronald Bonaparte, who was Napoleon's nephew, wrote two books about the Saami and had himself photographed in a Saami costume on his expedition in Lapland in 1884. In 1895 a play called *Les enfants du soleil de minuit* (The Children of the Midnight Sun) was performed in Paris; in it the actors sang, danced and played in a Saami setting under the guidance of some fake Saamis. In Helsinki the Saamis of Finnish Lapland held an extensive exhibition of their skills, customs and culture in 1910 and again in 1936. A documentary film was made to record the latter event.

At first, Saamis were taken to more southern parts of Europe to be exhibited as freaks, but in the late 19th century the nature of the exhibitions changed as the interest in folk cultures grew throughout Europe. There were four families, 33 reindeer and ten dogs in this travelling exhibition of Saamis in Halle in Germany in 1930.

were thought to contract diseases from the wind, water and the earth. The worst contagions, like smallpox, were called "God's plagues". Smallpox was incurable, but it could be prevented by burning juniper or drinking boiled water in which juniper had been steeped. When an infected person was visited, the cabin or *kota* (the tepee-like dwelling of the Saami) was fumigated by burning juniper twigs until it was full of smoke. Chewing pine gum was also considered to have a curative and prophylactic effect, while tar and water boiled with Labrador tea were also considered to be efficacious in curing many diseases. Tying a woollen thread around one's wrist or finger alleviated pain. This procedure was used as late as the twentieth century. Dried angelica and bear gall were also used, and people in those days believed in the curative powers of the waters from certain springs. As a cure for scurvy, a hot meat broth was boiled and blood and rye flour were added to it, or the patient might be given just blood to drink.

As reindeer herding became concentrated in the hands of an ever- decreasing number of persons in the nineteenth century, more and more Saamis became settler farmers. An English writer called Cutcliffe Hyne passed through Inari in the 1890s on a journey from northern Norway to Tornio and noted: "... The majority of the Lapps lived in snug wooden houses, tilled the ground, tended cattle, lived prosperous lives". An American traveller called Hudson Strode describes the Saamis that he met in the late 1930s in the following words: "They are becoming more like Finns in many ways. When they make money and build themselves good houses, they often begin to call themselves Finns".

LOGGING CAMPS

With the development of the wood and paper industry, the value of the forests began to rise rapidly from the 1860s on. At the same time, the first steam-driven sawmills were built in Finnish Lapland: Laitakari Sawmill in Kemi in 1861 and Röyttä Sawmill in Tornio in 1862. A much larger facility, Karihaara Sawmill was built by the Norwegian Terje Olsen in Kemi in 1873 and 1874. The increased amount of timber that this mill required was taken from further north in central Finnish Lapland. Thus the first logging camps came into being there. Forestry was to have a considerable importance for the economy of Lapland. The numbers of logs taken from the north rose to hundreds of thousands. Felling the trees at the source of the rivers in the roadless tracts of the wilderness and floating them downriver first to the sawmills and later to the paper mills at the mouth of the Kemi River provided jobs for the people of Finnish Lapland right up to the 1960s. And

Log-floating on the Kemi River in the early 20th century. The first logging camps were opened in Finnish Lapland in the 1860s. Log-floating quickly became an important source of income for the farming population, and it also brought a lot of new inhabitants to Lapland.

more manpower flowed in from southern Finland. It has been estimated that every winter there were about 10,000 men employed in forestry along the Kemi River. The work brought a gradual rise in the standard of living, and Finnish Lapland moved into the monetary age; throughout the nineteenth century, the economy of the north had been mainly self-sufficient or based on barter. Most of the profit from the logging accrued to the state, which owned the vast majority of the forests in Lapland, and to the timber companies. The rise of forestry also made Rovaniemi the main town in the province. The railway to Rovaniemi was completed in 1909, and this increased its significance as the new gateway to Lapland. The Oulu-Tornio line had been opened a little earlier, in 1903.

The industrial establishments of Finnish Lapland have concentrated in the Kemi-Tornio region. The oldest was a brewery called Torneå Bryggeri Aktiebolaget (it changed its name to Lapin Kulta Oy in 1969), which was established in Tornio in 1873. The first modern timber company, Trävaruaktiebolaget Kemi (Kemiyhtiö), was established in Kemi in 1893. In 1932 it received a competitor in a company founded by the state, Veitsiluoto Oy, which had begun sawmill and logging activities in Finnish Lapland in 1922. In 1913, the Kemiyhtiö company decided to build a chemical pulp mill, and this was completed in 1919. The company built a second chemical pulp mill in 1927. Veitsiluoto Oy began the production of pulp in 1930, likewise in Kemi. These two companies also brought the paper and board industry to Finnish Lapland in the 1950s. The northernmost factory in Finland is a mechanical pulp mill in Kemijärvi; it was opened in 1965.

Life in the logging camps was tough. In the early days, working and living conditions were miserable. The food was monotonous, and because of the long distances involved the loggers' social contacts with the local villages were meagre. There was no such thing as strict working hours, and particularly during the log-floating season in spring when there was no night the men worked around the clock. In order to better their conditions, the loggers founded their own organisation called *Pohjolan tukkityöläisten rengas* in 1906. Despite the poor conditions, there was a plentiful supply of manpower as logging paid better that other kinds of work. When the logging season was over, a great band of loggers gathered in Rovaniemi to celebrate and look for new employment. To quote the English writer Cutcliffe

A logging camp beside the Vaattunki River near Rovaniemi in 1929. The logging camps also offered women work as housekeepers.

Hyne again on Rovaniemi in the 1890s: "It was the most considerable place in the North, and the post-house was almost an hotel". When Hyne and his companions were investigating a great pile of reindeer antlers behind a certain shop, a crowd gathered round and laughed out loud at them; they could not understand what interest a pile of old bones could hold.

Mainly from the 1920s on, women were also working in the logging camps. They handled the catering and housekeeping tasks. Some of them were young girls, some were the wives or daughters of loggers working in the camps. Some of them even brought their small children with them. Usually, however, the camp housekeepers were young women, and they normally stayed in the job for a couple of years. Discipline in the camps was strict, which permitted the housekeepers to sleep undisturbed behind a curtain in a separate recess of the cabin.

A CORRIDOR TO THE ARCTIC OCEAN

After the frontier in the north between Finland and Norway was closed in 1852, the Finnish nationalist Fennoman movement began to criticise the legality of the frontier. One of the leaders of the Fennomans was Georg Zachris Forsman (nom-de-plume: Yrjö-Koskinen), who later became a professor of history. In 1868, he wrote that from the Finnish point of view it was a downright injustice that the passage of Finnish citizens to the Arctic Ocean had been cut off. As Finland had not been invited to the negotiating table in the frontier discussions, her interests had not been taken into account. In Yrjö-Koskinen's opinion, the blame for this lay with Norway, which, fearing that Russia would take her good harbours in the Varanger Peninsula, wished to avert this danger by defining her national frontier more strictly. Yrjö-Koskinen raised the question in his celebrated work *Oppikirja Suomen kansan historiasta* (A History Book of the Finnish People) published in 1869; it came to be the manifesto of the Fennoman movement and an incentive for national activism.

The debate about Finland's corridor to the Arctic Ocean became intense again in the 1880s. The matter was raised in the Diet in Helsinki by the editor-in-chief of *Helsingfors Dagbladet*, Robert Castrén, the son of the famous researcher Mathias Alexander Castrén. Robert Castrén pointed out that in 1864 the Tsar had promised a corridor to the Arctic Ocean in return for an area in the Karelian Isthmus in south-east Finland on which a rifle factory was located. Soon nearly twenty years would have passed since the promise, and nothing had happened. Castrén was concerned that the uncertain situation was causing a constant emigration of people from Finland to Norway and a depletion of Finnish Lapland's already sparse population. The question of a corridor to the Arctic Ocean was also raised in the government's official newssheet in January 1885 as well as in one of the country's leading newspapers, *Uusi Suometar*, which printed an extensive article

The Civil War waged between the left-wing Reds and the right-wing Whites from 28 January to 6 May 1918 is the most tragic event in the history of Finland. It was partly inspired by the Russian Revolution, but the poor food situation in the country also roused the proletariat to rise in rebellion.

Although the front line in the war ran across southern Finland between Tampere and Vaasa, leaving northern Finland on the White side, there too there were skirmishes in the larger communities. For example, there was a very active workers' association in Rovaniemi in the early twentieth century, and its activities became more radical as a result of the shortage of food in 1917. The workers called logging strikes on both the Kemi and Ounas Rivers. At the same time, the political right and centre closed ranks and armed themselves. In October 1917, the Reds of Rovaniemi established their own workers' guard and held a large public meeting. In November, they joined the rest of the country in a national strike. The situation became exacerbated when in the middle of January 1918 the Whites demanded that the small detachment of Russian troops garrisoned in the town be removed. This caused a scuffle between the Whites and the Reds. There was shooting in Rovaniemi, too, when war finally broke out at the end of January 1918. The Whites gained control of the town, and some of the Reds fled south, while others set off for Russia. When the war was over, the Whites initiated reprisals in northern Finland as they did elsewhere in the country.

Although hostilities in the north were not on the same scale as in southern Finland, there too people died as a result of fighting or executions. About 800 persons (2% of the total number of those who died in the war) lost their lives in the Province of Oulu, to which Finnish Lapland belonged at that time. The largest number of deaths (67) happened in the city of Oulu. No actual battles were fought in the municipalities of Finnish Lapland, although there were local skirmishes, for example, in Tornio, Kemi and Rovaniemi. The largest numbers of deaths in the Civil War in Lapland happened in Rovaniemi (32), the rural municipality of Kemi (32), Alatornio (25), Simo (19), Kemijärvi (16), Kemi (12) and Sodankylä (12). During the war there was a prisoner-of-war camp in Rovaniemi, in which a little under a hundred Red prisoners were held.

After the Finnish Civil War, the White victors made a number of incursions into the Olonets region and the Karelian border area of the Soviet Union, which they considered to be territory inhabited by Finnic peoples, in order to liberate them from the new Soviet system. These campaigns proved futile. One of them was made into the Pechenga area between April and June 1918. It was led by one Onni Laitinen, the municipal medical officer of Sodankylä and a teacher from Helsinki called Thorsten Renvall, who had previously made a scientific expedition in Lapland. The contingent consisted of just under 200 men, a motley crew, the youngest of whom was fifteen and the oldest seventy years of age. There was squabbling among the participants, and the expedition failed to achieve its objectives.

in November 1885 entitled "Our Quarrels with Sweden and Norway in Lapland". Both of these texts criticised Norway's intensifying nationalist policy, as a result of which the situation of the Finns who lived in northern Norway had deteriorated alarmingly.

Generally, the debate that was waged from the 1860s to the 1880s on a corridor to the Arctic Ocean can be regarded as an expression of the rising Finnish nationalist movement. It had considerable significance for the history of Finnish Lapland: the fact that the matter of access to the Arctic Ocean was taken up by the country's leading politicians is evidence that the farthest reaches of Lapland were now finally regarded as part of Finnish Finland, or at least that there was a desire to so regard them. Finland obtained her corridor to the Arctic Ocean in the form of a strip of territory on the coast of the Barents Sea in the Tartu Peace Treaty of 1920 with the Soviet Union.

ROVANIEMI BECOMES THE CAPITAL OF FINNISH LAPLAND

Like many other travellers, those who participated in these expeditions set off from Rovaniemi, which early in the 20th century began to grow into the main town in Finnish Lapland for communications, trade and services. The aspect and importance of the town changed even more when a decision was made in 1936 to make Finnish Lapland into a province of its own, and the provincial administration began operating from Rovaniemi in 1938. The people of Finnish Lapland had cherished idea of obtaining a province of their own for decades. In 1917, the project had advanced to a stage where a leaflet outlining a plan for the province was published. However, Rovaniemi's progress towards becoming the capital of the Province of Lapland was not all plain sailing, for Kemi, the main centre of industry in Lapland, also aspired to the same position. The rise of the village and municipality of Rovaniemi had begun with the first logging camps

A lodge was built on the Arctic Circle in 1950, since when it has been a destination for ever-increasing numbers of tourists. The picture shows a sleeve badge of Rovaniemi which emphasises the role of the town as the gateway to the Artic Circle and northern Lapland.

Thanks to the timber trade and the logging camps, Rovaniemi became the commercial centre of Finnish Lapland in the late 19th century. The picture is of the famous Rovaniemi Market in 1931.

Map 3. The Province of Lapland 1938

and sawmills. In 1870, the population of the municipality was about 4000. When the railway was extended there in 1909, the population rose to 11,000. The growth subsequently increased rapidly, and by 1940 there were 22,700 persons living in the area. As a result of this increase, Rovaniemi was made into a market town in 1928, and then it rapidly became the focus of the whole of northern Finnish

Lapland's trade and communications along with its educational establishments and the provincial administration. In the same year, the province's own newspaper *Lapin Kansa* was established there. In 1938, the total population of the province amounted to about 137,000.

The events of the Second World War in Finnish Lapland will be properly dealt with in the following chapter, but it is apposite to mention here that the war years saw a lively social life and strong economic growth in Rovaniemi. During the Winter War (1939–1940), the market town received foreign war correspondents, who lodged in the Pohjanhovi Hotel. At one time there were as many as forty or so foreign journalists in Rovaniemi. The local inhabitants were amused by one French newspaperman who arrived in the bitter frost wearing shorts and a beret. The correspondents visited the front lines and a field hospital. During the Continuation War (1941–44), the streets of the market town were filled with German soldiers; indeed the German presence was so marked that Rovaniemi began to be called a town of Germans. In January 1942 there were about 6000 Germans in Rovaniemi. The Germans set up their General Headquarters in the local schools and built barracks and stores in the vicinity of the town centre. They had their own officers' club, theatre, sports field, bookshop, motor repair garage, bakery, library and military hospital. In addition to that, they published their own newspaper, called *Lappland-Kurier*, and opened their own radio station. Rovaniemi was the centre of Finnish Lapland, but the lands to the north of it amazed the foreigners. In the late 1930s, a German forestry officer called Curt Strohmeyer wrote on reaching Sodankylä: "I take my baggage, and I imagine that I have escaped from culture. Or perhaps it is here that culture begins and civilisation ends."

The economy of Rovaniemi burgeoned during the Continuation War, for there was no lack of demand or purchasing power. In addition to the vitality brought by the presence of the Germans, the provincial capital acquired more and more central administrative organs and shops: it is indicative that in 1942 there were already as many as 43 shops in Rovaniemi. At the end of the war, Rovaniemi was burned by the Germans, and in 1946 a new town plan in the shape of reindeer antlers was drawn up by the renowned Finnish architect Alvar Aalto. Rovaniemi received its urban charter and became a city in 1960.

4

FINNISH LAPLAND IN THE SECOND WORLD WAR

THE MEN OF LAPLAND IN THE WINTER WAR

War was declared between Finland and the Soviet Union after the Soviets bombed Finnish territory on 30.11.1939. Throughout the summer and early autumn, people in the villages of Finnish Lapland had followed the news of the intensifying build-up of arms on the radio and in the papers. On 12 October 1939, the main paper of the region, *Lapin Kansa*, reported on the visit of Finnish negotiators to Moscow: "A crowd of several thousands saw off the Finnish delegation at Helsinki Railway Station as they set off for Moscow." The crown sang hymns and the national anthem. Another factor that increased tension between Finland and the Soviet Union was Germany's invasion of Poland on 1 September 1939 and its swift occupation of the country.

The glorious colours of autumn on Pallastunturi Fell. Pallasjärvi Lodge, which was built in 1934, is the oldest winter sports centre in Finnish Lapland. It has remained a popular resort right up to the present day.

72

A Saami yard beside the Könkämä River in Kilpisjärvi in 1939.

The Finnish High Command made no special arrangements in Lapland for the impending war. It was firmly believed that the Soviet Union would not launch an offensive in the north because of the poor communications there: "The distance to inhabited areas there is so great that they would inevitably face grave logistic problems before they reached any really important targets."

After the order for general mobilisation was issued, the men of Finnish Lapland assembled in their main villages on 13 October 1939. From there they travelled to an assembly camp in Kemi, where most of them had arrived by 19 October. The disposition of the men in Kemi lasted four days, after which they began group training. The training in Kemi lasted until 30 November, when it was interrupted by an air-raid warning at 1:05 p.m. The Winter War had started. After a week of fitting out, the main detachment of the Laplanders set off by train for the villages of Hyrynsalmi and Suomussalmi on the eastern border. They had their baptism of fire around 12 December, and these battles saw the first casualties from Lapland.

Battle conditions in the Winter War were extremely harsh: it was bitterly cold, and supplies did not get through after the desired fashion. Some of the men were badly frostbitten. The troops spent the Christmas of 1939 in the trenches. After Christmas they were moved to the Raate Road, Kuhmo and Löytövaara, scenes of some of the worst fighting in the war. At the front they had to sleep in the sub-zero temperatures in cardboard tents. The first men to go home on leave got their passes three and a half months after they had left. In early March, the fighting grew even fiercer, and a large number of men from Lapland fell in the snow along the frontier zone. The Soviet Union had rapidly occupied the whole region around Petsamo, and it had massed huge forces around the Kandalaksha area with the aim of cutting Finland in two. However, the Finns managed to repel the offensives. The bombardment by the enemy artillery on the morning of 13 March 1940 was the worst the men had experienced. But then suddenly, at 11 o'clock, silence fell, and somebody came running to announce that peace had been agreed.

In the Winter War there were volunteers from nearly every country in Europe fighting on the Finnish side. Most of them came from Sweden, 8000 men in all. There were about 700 Norwegians and a thousand Danes. There were approximately 300 Hungarians, while about 200 volunteers came from Britain and sixty from Estonia. In Italy, about 5000 men had volunteered, but a ban on people leaving the country was imposed there, and only a fraction of them ever reached Finland. There were also some individual volunteers from Belgium, Holland, France, the USA, Portugal and Ireland. In actual practice, the volunteers from outside Scandinavia shrank to about 200 men, from whom a special detachment was formed in 1940. They hardly had a taste of battle before the war ended.

The most significant contribution of the foreign volunteers was made by the Swedish and Norwegian volunteer army called *Svenska Frivilligkåren*. It was assigned a sector of the front around Salla in Lapland at the end of February 1940. The commander of the army, Lt. Col. Magnus Dyrsson, fell in the fighting. The Swedes also brought 25 fighter aircraft and pilots as well as an ambulance to Finland. Collections were made in Sweden, and in one a total of 1500 gold rings were donated.

Altogether 22,800 Finns fell in the Winter War, and 43,600 were wounded. The war dead from Lapland totalled 991 soldiers and 41 civilians. Not all the soldiers were demobilised after the war; most of them were kept on for further training. They only began to be discharged in May 1940. In the Winter War, Finland lost some of its territory in Lapland: the western side of the Rybachy Peninsula and the eastern part of the municipality of Salla.

RIGHT OF PASSAGE FOR THE GERMAN ARMY

The return to normality did not dim the Laplanders' memories of the Winter War, and the new developments in the international situation helped to keep them alive. Finland made peace with the Soviet Union in March 1940. At the same time, Germany began to occupy Norway, and relentlessly the world war came ever closer to Finnish Lapland. This changed Finland's whole strategic position. In the autumn of 1940, Finland began to negotiate about cooperation with Germany, which was interested in the Murmansk railway and the nickel

The inhabitants of Petsamo were originally Skolt Saamis. After its incorporation with Finland in 1920, Finnish influence in the area increased rapidly. The picture shows some local Saamis with their reindeer.

Pechenga becomes Petsamo

The Pechenga area was attached to Finnish Lapland under the name of Petsamo in 1920. It was about 10,400 sq. km in size, and it had approximately 1160 inhabitants, of whom about one third were Finns and a quarter Skolt Saamis. Finns had begun to move into the area from the 1850s on. The Skolts mainly lived in the Lapp Villages of Pechenga, Paatsjoki and Suonikylä. The Lapp Village was an administrative and social unit consisting of several usually interrelated families. The inhabitants of the Lapp Village of Pechenga lived beside the Pechenga River, those of the Paatsjoki Lapp Village along the banks of the Paats River, and the inhabitants of Suonikylä beside the Lutto River. The Skolts were nomads, changing their living place according to the seasons of the year. They were Orthodox in religion, having been converted in the sixteenth century, when a monastery was built in the area. The Petsamo area bordered on the Soviet Union with a joint border stretching from Korvatunturi Fell to

Some smallholdings in the village of Parkkina in the Petsamo region. There were determined attempts to extend agriculture as far as the coast of the Arctic Ocean.

the Arctic Ocean. The border with Norway ran along the Paats River, a 140-kilometre-long stream arising in Lake Inari and debouching into the Arctic Ocean. Its best-known rapids, Kolttaköngäs (Russian: Boris Gleb), was highly favoured by tourists.

After its attachment to Finland, a determined effort was made to make Petsamo Finnish, and this was rapidly achieved as Finns moved into the area. In 1929 its sixteen villages had 2300 inhabitants, of whom 53% were Finns, 17% Skolts, 3% other Saamis, 13% Russians, 13% Karelians and a few Komis and Norwegians. A law was passed in 1925 to induce people from Finland to settle in the Petsamo region by offering them land there. They were also attracted by the rich fishing that the area offered. When the Winter War broke out, the population of Petsamo was over 5000. It is indicative of the social make-up of the inhabitants that left- and right-wing parties received equal support in elections there.

The elementary schools played a major role in making the region Finnish. Elementary schools were established in Parkkina, Salmijärvi and Pummanki in 1921 and it was not long before the other larger villages got their own schools. Three agricultural societies, a workers' association, a gymnastics and sports club and a fishing club were also rapidly founded in the area. Postal services were likewise improved by establishing post offices and telephone exchanges. In this way the region was integrated more closely into Finland. There were already eight inns operating in the region in the late 1920s. These inns and the hotels that were to be built were important as the so-called Arctic Ocean Road from Rovaniemi to Petsamo was constructed in 1931, and this brought tourists to the area. The rapid development of tourism there is indicated by the fact that the Finnish company Aero began regular flights from Helsinki to Petsamo in 1940.

Finland was particularly interested in Petsamo's harbour, which did not freeze over in the winter, and its rich fishing waters as well as in the nickel deposits that had been discovered on Kaulatunturi and Kammikivitunturi Fells by Alppi Talvia and Hugo Törnqvist in the spring of 1921.

The Geological Survey of Finland had sent them to survey the iron content of the earth there. The multinational International Nickel Company of Canada Ltd. started mining for nickel in 1936.

In 1944 Finland lost the region to the Soviet Union, and it was re-named Pechenga again. Subsequently two large Russian mining towns, Nikel and Zapolyarny, were built there, and the population rose to approximately 47,000. The Finns were evacuated from Petsamo during the war and relocated in various parts of Finland. Many old inhabitants of Petsamo still vividly recall the region, which was eventually opened to tourists in the 1990s. Numerous books about Petsamo were published already in the 1920s, poems and songs were composed about it, and its natural beauty inspired many artists. The Swedish-speaking Finnish writer, Håkan Mörne, described the northern border region between Finland and the Soviet Union in the late 1930s as follows: "The Petsamo region is separated from the Soviet state by an artificial border, on each side of which the countryside is much the same." Despite this apparent similarity, however, the frontier was strictly guarded, as it was feared that spies used this northern route. An Englishman who travelled to Petsamo and accidentally strayed over the border was arrested in consequence. It took weeks before he got back to Britain by way of Arkhangelsk, Moscow and Helsinki.

of Petsamo. The nearer Germany's plans for an attack against the Soviet Union came to completion, the more important was the strategic position that northern Finland assumed as one of the bases from which to launch an offensive. Finland was driven to the negotiating table with Germany by the fear that she would have to face the Soviet Union alone once a new war broke out. The Germans' successful *Blitzkrieg* against Poland, Denmark, Holland, Belgium and lastly northern Norway had not passed unnoticed by the Finns, who believed that, if a war broke out between Germany and the Soviet Union, the former would emerge victorious.

The Finns were also rankled by the territorial losses they had sustained as a result of the Winter War: the country had been forced to surrender an economically important area of Karelia and part of the municipality of Salla in Lapland. On the other hand, the Soviet Union had voluntarily returned to Finland the Petsamo area, which it had swiftly occupied, apart from the Rybachy Peninsula. The peace conditions also obliged Finland to build a railway from the eastern frontier to Kemijärvi. This made Lapland vulnerable to quick occupation if war broke out. Apart from the new borders imposed by the Winter War, the Finns' pro-German sympathies were inspired by hopes of deals for the supply of food and weapons, to which Germany subsequently committed itself.

The negotiations between the Finns and the Germans proceeded to a point where, in September 1940, they entered into a military agreement that was to have far-reaching consequences for the history of Finland. On the basis of this agreement, the Finnish government accorded German troops the right of passage through Lapland from the ports on the Gulf of Bothnia to Petsamo and Kirkenes on the coast of the Arctic Ocean and back. The first German vessel, the *Biwi*, arrived in Vaasa harbour in the night of 22 September 1940 to the surprise of the locals and the authorities alike. The German troops were transported by train to Rovaniemi, from where they continued due north along the Arctic Ocean Road in motor vehicles. In accordance with an extension to the right-of-passage agreement, accommodation was built for 500 German soldiers in Sodankylä. The locals were mainly favourably disposed towards the Germans. Barracks were also built in Ivalo. Altogether over 10,000 German soldiers passed through Finnish

During the Continuation War (1941–44), the number of German soldiers in Finnish Lapland amounted at its highest to about 220,000. The picture shows German forces crossing the Petsamo border river in the early days of the war on 26 June 1941.

Lapland in the last months of 1940, and the number increased constantly during the following spring.

Finland's strategic position changed dramatically in early 1941, when the Soviet Union repeated its demand for the joint British and Canadian nickel mining company to be changed into a Russian and Finnish one. This raised the threat of war. The so-called "nickel crisis" divided Finnish opinion to the extent that the Finnish Ambassador in Moscow, Juho Kusti Paasikivi, who later became President of Finland, suggested that the Petsamo region should be surrendered altogether in exchange for other territory, but the Commander-in-Chief of the Finnish armed forces, Marshal C. G. E. Mannerheim, was in favour of a firmer line, and Germany also urged Finland to stay put in Petsamo. The inflamed situation was immediately reflected in Lapland. In February, the Chief-of-Staff of the German Army in Norway, Col. Erich Buschenhagen, came to Finland, travelling from Helsinki to Lapland, where he made a reconnaissance visit to the eastern border with the Soviet Union. The future commander of the German forces in Lapland, Gen. Eduard Dietl, also visited the province. They both travelled in civilian dress.

In spring 1941, the prospect of war breaking out began to be firmly entrenched, at least in the minds of the military. With the advent of summer, Finnish-German cooperation intensified. For example, on 7 June the inhabitants of the village of Vuotso in the municipality of Sodankylä were surprised by the arrival of the SS Nord division from Kirkenes in northern Norway. After overnighting in the village, the Germans continued on their way to Rovaniemi. In that month there were already 40,600 German troops in Finnish Lapland and the northern part of the Province of Oulu, and their strength grew over the next three years to reach 220,000 in the autumn of 1944. At that time, the population of the Province of Lapland was only a little over 150,000. Lapland was a surprise to many of the Germans: they had expected to find there primitive people herding their reindeer. One German soldier recalled his surprise on arriving in Rovaniemi as follows: "Charming girls in flower-bedecked straw hats, billowing summer dresses and smart high-heeled shoes strolled along the tidy streets. The town was amazing." According to a German appraisal, their arrival in Rovaniemi was greeted with pleasure and enthusiasm by the Finnish officer corps, and this was reflected in the parties the latter organised in honour of the German troops.

LAPLAND COMES UNDER
GERMAN MILITARY ADMINISTRATION

By 1941 the whole of the Province of Lapland and the northernmost part of the Province of Oulu had been made into a German military administrative district with the agreement of the Finnish government after Risto Ryti, the President of Finland, and the Finnish Parliament had ratified the results of negotiations between the Finns and the Germans. Although war was imminent, no measures were undertaken to evacuate the population of Lapland. The civilian administration of the region was in the hands of the provincial government in Rovaniemi.

A new war, which became known in Finland as the "Continuation War", broke out between the latter and the Soviet Union on 25 June 1941. Germany had launched an offensive against the USSR three days earlier. The men of Lapland had been initially placed under the command of the Germans, and they had been sent off to the Salla front on 19 June. They arrived at the Soviet frontier three days later. Their objective was Kandalaksha town and particularly the Murmansk railway line. After a week's fighting, they re-conquered the area of Salla that Finland had lost in the Winter War as well as the adjacent village of Alakurtti. However, their losses in the notorious battle of Nurmitunturi Fell were frighteningly high.

When the advance of the Finnish-German forces became bogged down both on the Salla front and in Petsamo, the Finns' confidence in the fighting ability of the German troops began to waver. After the fierce battles of early autumn, the front lines became fixed, and the Germans' assurance of a swift march to the Murmansk railway remained an empty promise. In fact, they never reached the railway during the whole course of the war. The Laplanders claimed that the Germans did not know how to travel in the wilderness: they could not ski, nor orientate themselves nor move silently with their rattling equipment. The Germans' losses were high. In spring 1942, discipline among the men began to slip, and there were desertions and disobedience. In December 1941, the division formed by the men of Lapland was put under Finnish command and transferred to the Karelian front, and the disputes that had arisen when they were under joint command ended. From then on until autumn 1944, the defence of Lapland was the responsibility of the Germans alone. The Laplanders were sent to sectors of the front further south, and this aroused a certain amount of grievance and jealousy among them; while they were fighting far away in the south, their wives, daughters and sisters had to do with foreign soldiers.

Throughout the war, relations between the civilian population of Lapland and the German troops remained fairly good. The Germans offered the women a lot of well paid work, the barter economy flourished, romantic liaisons were formed, and children were born out of them. It has been estimated that during the Continuation War just under a thousand children were born of German soldiers in Finnish Lapland, a very low figure when compared with those of the occupied countries of Norway and Denmark. In the former, the figure has been estimated at 8000–10,000 and in the latter at 5600.

The association of young women with German soldiers was not always well regarded in the countryside in Lapland. In many cases, the girls were enticed into relationships with alcohol, sweets, coffee, cigarettes and other gifts. The critical attitude was often inspired by Christian considerations: premarital relations were not approved of. Most critical was the older population. From 1942 on, the criticism increased as Germany's success in the war declined. The Germans' presence in Lapland was regarded with most suspicion by the political left; the communists had strong support in the province.

Although generally the brotherhood of arms between the Finns and Germans went well, and discipline among the latter was strict, about sixty crimes of violence by them were registered during the war, most of them in 1943, when the initial enthusiasm for the alliance had waned along with German defeats. In addition to these crimes of violence, German soldiers committed acts of theft and high-handedness, such as shooting reindeer illegally, cutting down trees or levying taxes on gardens and potato fields.

Many German soldiers became frustrated in the wildernesses of Lapland. An Italian war correspondent called Curzio Malaparte spent the years 1941–43 in Finland, and he visited the front in Lapland. Of the morale among the German troops he wrote: "The war was far away from us. We were outside it, in a remote part of the world, in a timeless state, beyond humanity … They spoke of the war as of an old, distant matter, in their minds a secret resentment and a contempt for acts of violence, hunger, depredations and mass murders … An Alpine light infantry patrol approached me, their faces covered by mosquito nets. It was one of the many patrols, specially trained for guerrilla warfare in the Arctic forests, that ranged over the fells and forests of the Ivalo and Inari regions, ambushing Norwegian and Russian partisans." His views were echoed by many German war correspondents: "A wilderness on which a human foot has hardly stepped has become our battle terrain. Civilisation, houses, people in ordinary clothes have become remote, unreal concepts for us."

Map 4.
Lapland
during the
Conti-
nuation
War
(1941–
1944)

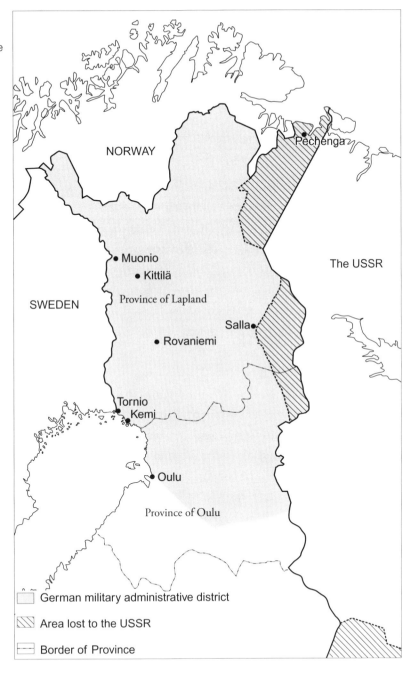

NORWAY

Pechenga

The USSR

● Muonio

● Kittilä

Province of Lapland

Salla●

● Rovaniemi

SWEDEN

Tornio
Kemi●

● Oulu

Province of Oulu

German military administrative district

Area lost to the USSR

Border of Province

CIVILIAN MURDERS AND PRISON CAMPS

During the Continuation War, the Soviet Union sent detachments of partisans over the border into Finland, and as a result of their activities altogether about 170 civilians died in the frontier zone. The size of the detachments varied from a score or so of men to a couple of hundred. The partisans were particularly active in the summer months between 1942 and 1944. The Finns estimated that in the summer of 1943 there were about eighteen groups comprising some 1700 men operating in Finland. The partisans made attacks on eight targets in Finnish Lapland. In the summer of 1944, they raided Seitajärvi in the municipality of Savukoski, where they executed eleven women and children. They also attacked the village of Kuosku in the same municipality. In the summer of 1943, the partisans also attacked the post van and an inn in Laanila on the border between Sodankylä and Inari, killing Bishop Yrjö Vallinmaa, who was travelling from his see in Oulu. In Yliluiro in the same area, attacks were made on individual farms, and five women and children lost their lives. There were also attacks in Niemelä and Hautajärvi in the municipality of Salla. In a strike on Lokka in the municipality of Sodankylä in July 1944, 21 women, children and old persons were shot. Altogether about seventy civilians died in Finnish Lapland during the Continuation War.

People also died in the Finnish prison camps in Lapland, of which there were two: Camp no. 9 in Kemi and Camp no. 8 in Ivalo. The central camp in Kemi had subsidiary camps in Rovaniemi, Kemijärvi and Sodankylä, while Ivalo camp had a subsidiary camp at Kolosjoki in the Petsamo area. The operating principle of the camps was simple: individual employers purchased labour from them, for which they paid them an agreed sum. The prisoners, who might be Finns or Russians, could be sent to work all over Finnish Lapland. Prisoner labour was purchased for logging work, for example by Lapland's big timber companies, Veitsiluoto and Kemijoki and by the National Board of Forestry. There were several logging camps manned by prisoners at the head waters of the Kihinen and the Luiro Rivers in Sodankylä. Individuals could also hire prisoners to do repairs or agricultural work. The prisoners were guarded by men who had been slightly disabled at the front.

The Germans used a lot of prisoner labour in Lapland. Germany's road-building and construction programme during the war was administered by *Organization*

Todt, which had a subsidiary department in Finland called *Einsatz Finnland* (Operation Finland). Most of the Germans in Finland operated in Lapland, so *Organization Todt* had its work sites in the north too. The first task was to build a railway line from Rovaniemi to Petsamo, but the project subsequently fell through. However, the organisation concentrated on building roads and repairing the existing poor ones in Lapland, strengthening the work force at the power station on the Jäniskoski Rapids in Petsamo, building barracks and organising forestry work. The operating principle of *Organization Todt* was that the work should be done by foreigners, mainly prisoners. For example, in November 1942 there were about 700

Petsamo (Russian: Pechenga) belonged to Finland between 1920 and 1944. It rapidly became a popular tourist destination for trekkers and anglers. This old postcard shows Jäniskoski Rapids on the Paats River in the Petsamo region.

Russian prisoners-of-war working in the Kaamanen-Karigasniemi road-building gangs. Prisoners of various nationalities were also brought from central Europe, but their numbers decreased as there began to be enough Russian prisoners. The prisoners' food was miserable, they were harshly treated, and mortality in the camps was high. There were several German prisoner-of-war camps in Lapland: for example, there were three in Tankavaara in Sodankylä, in which 1000–1500 captured Russians were held.

THE LAPLAND WAR AND EVACUATION

The war between Finland and the Soviet Union ended with a truce on 4 September 1944. Finland was required to make territorial concessions and to pay considerable war reparations. Lapland lost the whole of the Petsamo region and part of Salla to the USSR, which also demanded that Finland expel the over 220,000 German troops in the country within two weeks. This was an impossible task. The Finns had to drive out their former brothers-in arms by force. The first shots were fired in what was called the "Lapland War" on 28 September 1944 at Pudasjärvi in the Province of Oulu. Just over a week later, on 6 October, the war was in full swing in Tornio and on the following day in Kemi. The Germans began to withdraw rapidly towards the north along the Arctic Ocean Road and the road to Kilpisjärvi. On 9 October, Lothar Rendulic, who had succeeded Eduard Dietl as commander-in-chief of the German forces in Lapland, issued an order to burn all the government buildings in Rovaniemi. A few days later, the order was extended, and the Germans torched all the houses in the villages along the roads. They also blew up all the bridges and mined the roads. The reasons for the Germans' burning of Lapland was partly inspired by revenge but also dictated by the scorched earth tactic frequently used in war; destroying the bridges and roads and burning the houses effectively slowed down the progress of a pursuing enemy.

Before the Lapland War began, the Germans had constructed fortifications at Tankavaara in Sodankylä in order to defend the Petsamo nickel mines against an attack from the south and at the same time to protect their road communications to northern Norway. The Battle of Tankavaara (29–30 October 1944) was a short one, for the Germans wished to spare their troops. They slipped away towards the

A view of Valtakatu Street in Rovaniemi taken on 19 October 1944, after the town was burned by the Germans. The Lapland War between the Finns and the Germans lasted from the autumn of 1944 to the spring of the following year. When they withdrew from Finnish Lapland, the Germans destroyed most of the buildings there.

Arctic Ocean under cover of darkness. The last German soldiers left Finland on 27 April 1945. The Germans also built another fortification, the *Sturmbock-Stellung* at Jämärä in the municipality of Kilpisjärvi. It has subsequently been renovated into a tourist attraction.

In the Lapland War, 772 Finns fell, 262 disappeared and 2904 were wounded. German losses amounted to about 4500 men. Altogether the number of Finns

who died, disappeared or fell in the Continuation War and the Lapland War was high, approximately 208,000 men. Of these, 2552 came from Lapland; indeed the province of Lapland suffered badly, losing a proportionally higher number of men than any other province. The worst losses were incurred in the fighting around Nurmitunturi Fell in the municipality of Salla in autumn 1941.

When news of the truce between Finland and the Soviet Union reached Lapland, it caused consternation among the people. The region was full of German troops, and the people believed that the USSR would now move its own forces there. On the radio and in the press, the authorities issued an order on 8 September 1944 for the whole population of Finnish Lapland to be evacuated. The evacuations began immediately. The people were first taken to Rovaniemi, and from there they were transported by rail either to Ostrobothnia in western Finland or by way of Tornio and Haparanda to Sweden. In the beginning, the Germans allowed their motor vehicles to be used for evacuating the people, who were ordered to leave the goods they were taking with them by the roadside for later collection. With them they were only allowed to take their most important possessions and three days' food supplies. The goods left at the roadsides were never picked up, and the Germans burned them together with the houses. In total 111,000 persons were evacuated from Finnish Lapland. In addition to these, about 250 Finnish women left with German soldiers.

Sweden had promised to take 100,000 evacuees and their cattle. During the Continuation War, 70,000 children had been evacuated there, about 12,000 of whom remained permanently in the country. According to the evacuation order, the border crossing point was Haparanda, but in practice, people crossed the Torne and Muonio frontier rivers at ten different points. On the Swedish side, there were five assembly areas to receive the evacuees from Finnish Lapland. The first trains arrived in Haparanda on 16 January 1944 filled with 2300 evacuees.

Finnish soldiers hoisting the Finnish flag after the war in 1945 near Lake Kilpisjärvi at a point where the frontiers of three states (Finland, Norway and Sweden) meet.

In the assembly areas, the evacuees were examined, sent to sauna and given food and clothes. Then they were divided up and sent to 600 different camps, mainly in the provinces of Norrbotten, Västerbotten and Västernorrland. Some of the camps were large, whole villages holding over a thousand inmates, like the Lindå camp (nicknamed "Little Rovaniemi") at Jörn in Västerbotten. Others were small communities of only a few dozen persons. The worst problems arose in the large camps, like the Vilhelmina and Dorotea camps, where small children were carried off by epidemics. Despite these setbacks, people who had suffered the stress of several years of war gladly received the accommodation, heating and food offered in Sweden: for many it was as if they had arrived in paradise.

In Ostrobothnia, the evacuees from Lapland were mainly located in villages in the Province of Vaasa. They excitedly followed what was happening in the Lapland War, and when it finally ended, some of them fled back home prematurely. The region was heavily mined, and the authorities had only given permission for the men to return, for they were urgently required to work in the forests. Finally, in the summer of 1945, the all-clear was given for the evacuees in Sweden and the families in Ostrobothnia to go back. But even then, and for a long time to come after the war, dozens of people in the region were killed or maimed by mines.

When the evacuees returned home after their trying journey, they were greeted by a miserable scene: all that was left standing in the villages were some blackened chimney stacks. However, the inhabitants quickly began to put up saunas and outbuildings, and by the autumn most of them had a small cabin in which to start their lives afresh.

AID FOR LAPLAND

Foreign organisations and states provided active support for the rebuilding of Finnish Lapland. When the population returned there, Sweden gave appreciable assistance in organising transportation, clothes, foodstuffs and temporary accommodation. Even before the Lapland War, in September 1944, a Foreign Aid Committee had been established to coordinate all foreign aid coming to Finland from abroad. In the early autumn of 1945, aid began to come in from a Quaker organisation called the American Friends Service Committee. It was through this organisation, for example, that assistance from the Pope to provide shoes for the children of the ravaged eastern part of the Province of Oulu was distributed. And the United Nations Relief and Rehabilitation Administration (UNRRA) also began to send assistance to Lapland.

The organisations Help Finland Inc. and United Finnish Relief, which were supported by Finnish immigrants in America, participated in the American Quakers' aid activities. Through them tons of parcels of clothes, shoes, domestic goods, blankets, etc. were sent to Finland. The aid from the American Finns was focussed mainly on the Rovaniemi area and Kittilä and Sodankylä in central Lapland, in other words, those areas that had suffered most from the ravages of war. The Quakers had their own office in Rovaniemi, and the local representatives of the Red Cross helped them in distributing the aid to the most needy. When the UNRRA aid began to arrive in Lapland in 1946, the Quakers turned the focus of their effort to central Finland.

The UNRRA assistance, too, was very concrete. The goods the organisation sent to Lapland could be redeemed with food ration cards. The most commonly distributed goods were flour, sugar and cod-liver oil. Of the domestic articles sent, frying pans and buckets were most in demand; the evacuees had been obliged to leave with only small carrier bags, so when they returned they had to acquire all their domestic articles anew. The assistance provided by UNRRA was thus very important. Assistance was also provided in organising health care and acquiring machines. Money grants were paid to war widows and their families, and support was provided for house building and repairs.

A considerable amount of assistance was also sent to Finnish Lapland by Sweden and the other Scandinavian countries. The Red Cross organisations of various countries sent medicine, baby packs, clothes, etc., and two ambulances were also donated. Sweden gave nursing packs, rubber boots, over a hundred cows as well as money to build clinics. UNICEF also sent material assistance to the area. The aid continued to come in until the early 1950s. It was certainly needed, for 70–90% of the buildings in the Province of Lapland had been destroyed. The worst affected areas were the villages along the main roads and the eastern frontier. In addition to a severe lack of materials, another factor that made it difficult for people to start up again was the fact that the stocks of reindeer had been depleted by about 20,000 animals in the war and those of domestic animals by 25,000.

The people of Lapland got rid of the psychological traumas caused by the war in work and home-making: nativity figures in Lapland after the war were the highest in the country. The experiences of the war were hardest for those men who had spent their youth fighting in it, and they released their tensions by establishing farms in the wilderness, drying out wide expanses of swampland, toiling in the logging camps and occasionally resorting to drink.

This arm badge displays the crest of the municipality of Inari, which is symbolised by Lake Inari and the midnight sun.

Samii Litto

Samii Litto was the first civic organisation founded by the Saami themselves. It was established in April 1945 in Alavieska in Ostrobothnia, where some of the Saami population of Lapland had been evacuated. Before that, in 1932, some friends of Lapland in Helsinki had founded the Society for the Promotion of Saami Culture, which published a Saami-language journal called *Sábmelaš* and together with *Samii Litto* pressurised the Finnish government into establishing a Committee for Saami Affairs in 1949. Other achievements of *Samii Litto* were the establishment of the Christian Folk High School for Saamis in Inari in 1952 and the foundation of the Saami Museum in 1959; it was opened to the public in Inari in 1962. It has subsequently been replaced by the modern Siida Museum, which was opened in 2000. The old museum area still functions as an open-air museum.

Samii Litto opened its own office in Inari in the late 1940s, and it established branches in the villages at the same time. It had taken organisations in Norway and Sweden as its models. The first Saami association in Sweden, *Vilhelmina-Åsele*, was founded in 1904, and the first one in Norway two years later. The first national Saami Conference was held in Sweden in 1919 and in Norway the following year. Before that, in February 1917, Swedish and Norwegian Saamis had assembled for the first Pan-Nordic Saami Conference in Trondheim.

After the war, the position of the Saami began to improve. The Saami Council was established in Finland in 1956, the Advisory Committee for Saami Affairs in 1960, the Saami Delegation in 1973 and in 1995 the Saami Parliament. In the following year, the principle of cultural self-determination for the Saami was officially adopted. The ILO Convention on Indigenous and Tribal Peoples in independent countries was ratified in Finland in 1989.

In the 1980s and 1990s, the Saami ethnopolitical movement put strong pressure on the government of Finland to settle questions relating to the land rights of the Saami. The organisations defending Saami interests believe that the Finnish state should return to the Saami the pastures that were appropriated by the Crown in the days of Swedish rule. So far this demand has not received the response sought by the Saami. There have also been disputes between the Saami and those persons who have Saami forebears (the so-called "Lapps"), for example about who has the right to vote in elections for the Saami Parliament.

In 2005 there were about 7000 Saamis in Finland, of whom 4000 live in the Province of Lapland. Of the Nordic countries, Norway has the highest Saami population (over 40,000), while there are over 20,000 Saamis living in Sweden and about 2000 in Russia.

5

POWER STATIONS AND
RESERVOIRS

THE BOOK OF LAPLAND

After the war, there was a growing need for the various regions in Finland to create profiles for themselves and to inculcate a feeling of affiliation among their inhabitants by strengthening their regional awareness. This was certainly true of Lapland, and one example of it was the publication of a work entitled *Lapin kirja* (The Book of Lapland) in 1956. It was specifically targeted at the schoolchildren of the region. The Provincial Governor, Uuno Hannula, began this regional guide by emphasizing the size of the province: "Do you know how big the Province of Lapland actually is? If we claim that it's as big as three European countries together, you may doubt it. But it's true: the combined area of Belgium, Holland and Switzerland is 105,962 square kilometres, and that of the Province of Lapland 99,130 square kilometres. There's not a big difference."

At that time, the population of Finnish Lapland was growing, and people looked to the future with confidence. The forests were full of timber, the rapids provided

Isohaara Power Station, built in 1949, was the first on the Kemi River. The process of harnessing the Kemi, the longest river in Finland, began in the 1940s.

electricity, the swamps could be drained and turned into fields, and undiscovered mineral deposits were thought to reside in the hills and fells: "This is the land of the future, this northern region of ours."

All the leading cultural personalities of Lapland in the 1950s contributed to the book. It represented the Saami and Finnish history and culture of the region on an equal basis for the first time. Along with the stories and historical facts, there were numerous poems, the lyrics of Saami chants and riddles, and there were brief descriptions of each of the municipalities in the province. For example, Enontekiö is mentioned as having the highest fell (Halti, 1254 m), Inari as the land of gold prospectors, and Karunki beside the Torne River as the "Salmon Parish". There was a poem about Kemi and its factories, while Kittilä was remembered as the place where the torch for the Helsinki Olympic Games was ignited with the rays of the midnight sun in July 1952. Savukoski was presented as the home of Santa Claus, Tornio as the port through which goods from Europe were imported, and Utsjoki as the land of the nomadic reindeer herders. "Lapland is a land of great contrasts: here the bright nights of summer and the long darkness of winter meet. But every season has its own beauty: the glorious colours of autumn on the fells, the splendour of the Northern Lights in the winter sky, the light of the sun on the snow in spring and after it all the short but lovely summer. What more could a person wish for?"

THE HARNESSING OF THE KEMI RIVER

In fact, however, this picture of the idyllic, untouched nature of Lapland was no longer true. With the territory that Finland lost to the Soviet Union as a consequence of the Second World War went one third of the country's hydro-electric power plants. At the same time, the manufacture of the industrial goods that the Soviet Union required to be paid as war reparations caused a considerable increase in the demand for energy. In this situation, the authorities turned their gaze to the great rivers, the Oulu and the Kemi, that still flowed unharnessed in northern Finland. It has been pointed out that the decision to harness these rivers was prompted not only by the afore-mentioned energy requirements that resulted from the Continuation War but also by "the attempt to obtain private gain and

Schoolchildren from Karesuvanto seeing the sights in Helsinki in 1957. The children are posing on the steps of the Cathedral in Senate Square.

A new church was built in Salla in 1950 to replace the one destroyed in the war. It was designed by Eero Eerikäinen and Osmo Sipari. The Parish of Salla received financial support for this project from the Danish Lutheran Church.

power through exploiting the crisis and the arrogant desire of the engineers to show just what modern technology could do, whether it be nature, the law or the ordinary peasant that stood in its way".

The decision to harness the Oulu River was made in 1940, and the first power station on the Kemi River, Isohaara, began operating in 1949. Before that, the country's leading paper industry concerns had started buying up sections of the latter river where there were rapids. Their agents went along the river in horse-drawn carts and swiftly bought for cash all the stretches of the river where there were rapids between Rovaniemi and Kemijärvi. The industrialists who dreamt of possessing the hydro-power resources of the north joined forces and founded a company called Pohjolan Voima Oy in 1943. After the Lapland War they reached an agreement with the government, and the company was granted permission to build an earth dam with a railway line and a road running across it on the spot where the Germans had blown up the Kemi Bridge. Thus the construction of Isohaara Power Station began. The dam was completed in the spring of 1946. The obtaining of building permission had been made easier by the fact that the decisions spoke all the time of temporary permits. In the early stages of the harnessing of the Kemi River, the directors of Pohjolan Voima were supported by the Governor of the Province of Lapland, Kaarlo Hillilä. The state also actively supported the construction of the power stations by granting millions of Finnish marks in loans.

In order to realise the power station projects, Kemijoki Oy, a company in which the state owned a majority of the shares, was established in 1952, and construction work on the largest power station on the Kemi River, Petäjäskoski, commenced the following year. In addition to the power stations, two large reservoirs, Lokka and Porttipahta, were built at the headwaters of the Kemi River in the municipality of Sodankylä. The building of the Lokka reservoir meant that two of the villages of the Sompio area, Korvanen and Riesto, were completely submerged under the water, as were parts of two others, Mutenia and Lokka. About 600 people were forced to move, mainly to the nearby village of Vuotso or to the main village of Sodankylä. The construction of the Lokka reservoir caused an uproar in the press. The area had not been cleared before it was covered with water, and as a result the water smelt of rotting trees and undergrowth. "Lokka Stinks" wrote the local paper. When

The naivist paintings of Andreas Alariesto, a self-taught artist from Sodankylä, attracted a lot of attention in Finnish art circles in the 1970s. This work *Reindeer and a Lapp in Summer* was painted in 1976.

Porttipahta's turn came, the builders tried to solve the problem by clearing the area before letting in the water. The inhabitants of the villages that were submerged were practically forced to move to their new locations, although their willingness to do so was increased by the fact that they received monetary compensation from the state. In retrospect, however, the money was a small recompense for the loss of their trout streams, berry-picking areas, reindeer pastures and their familiar home surroundings. Contrary to expectations, the reservoirs subsequently turned out to be profitable for the people of central Lapland as fishing waters. Altogether

Andreas Alariesto

The life of the demolished and sunken villages of Sompio survived in ethnological descriptions, the best-known of which were written by the Finnish scholars of Lapland, Samuli Paulaharju and T. I. Itkonen. Itkonen's most celebrated work is probably *Suomen Lappalaiset* I and II (The Lapps of Finland), published in 1948. Paulaharju's extensive series of works on Lapland includes *Taka-Lappi* (Hinter-Lapland, 1927), *Kolttain mailla* (In the Land of the Skolts, 1921) and *Lapin muisteluksia* (Recollections of Lapland, 1922). Other valuable sources for the history of the Sompio area are to be found in the stories and paintings of its own son, Andreas Alariesto. Alariesto was born in December 1900 in the village of Riesto beside the Luiro River. Riesto, which lay at a distance of about seventy kilometres from the main village of Sodankylä, had a long history: it was mentioned as a village as early as the sixteenth century. The terrain consists mainly of marshy lowlands, but in the north looms the Saariselkä fell district, with Nattanen and Raututunturi Fells prominent. At the time when Alariesto was born, the people got a living from small-scale cattle farming, reindeer herding, hunting and fishing, in other words, the typical mixed economy of Lapland. Culturally, the area represents a border between two cultures: the Finnish and the Saami. Alariesto was himself of Finnish pioneer settler stock, but he lived in an area traditionally inhabited by the Saami. This background clearly provided the foundation for the multicultural identity of central Lapland that he created in his pictures and tales.

Alariesto became famous for his naïve paintings, which were in fact depictions of the folk tales of the region. His productivity increased in the 1960s, a decade of great change in Lapland. All that was old seemed to be disappearing in the path of the new, and he felt that it was important to record the "old Lapland" for future generations. The stories are mostly set at the turn of the nineteenth and twentieth centuries. He came to national prominence in 1975 with an exhibition he held in Kunsthalle Helsinki. Unlike the art of Lapland of the 1920s and 1930s, in which landscapes dominated, Alariesto depicted people, animals and events. His technique was always to paint the event first and only then the landscape "in the space that was left".

Andreas Alariesto started working at the age of sixteen building the main road to Ivalo. When the Civil War broke out, he set off, like many other young men from Sompio, for Russia, where he joined the Murmansk Finnish Legion, which formed part of the British Army. When the First World War ended, this foreign legion of about 1200 men was sent back to Finland in handcuffs. Alariesto was convicted of treason and sentenced to six years hard labour. However, the sentence was commuted to a probationary one, and he was permitted to return to Lapland. He worked for a while as a log floater and logger, but then he set off again for Petsamo. He took a job as head porter in a tourist hotel. In the eight years he spent there, he depicted the magnificent rugged scenery of Petsamo; now the landscape too became the subject of his pictures.

In Petsamo, Alariesto met artists from southern Finland, and from them he learnt how to use oils. His creative powers burgeoned, and he painted, photographed, composed song lyrics, stuffed birds and made tourist souvenirs from starfish, crayfish and whalebones. The war interrupted this inspired period in Petsamo, and in it his pre-war works were destroyed. The Petsamo period also ended somewhat unfortunately for him in that he was arrested by the Finnish Security Police and interrogated under suspicion of spying for the Russians. However, he was acquitted and sent to the front in the Winter War.

Many felt that the laying waste of Finnish Lapland in the war also destroyed the exotic land of myth that Lapland had been. For example, the celebrated ethnographer of Lapland, T. I. Itkonen, no longer wished to return to the ravaged land. The destruction of Lapland and the loss of Petsamo to Russia after the war were background factors in Alariesto's recording work. It was necessary to preserve what could still be salvaged: the legends of the old Lapland. He was also prompted by the harnessing of the Kemi River and the inundation of his home village of Riesto under the Lokka reservoir to transmit the stories he had heard as a child in the medium of paint. Alariesto defended his work, claiming: "Art must not be the prerogative of a few." Before he died in 1989, he donated 64 of his works to his home municipality. The modern tourist can view them in the Alariesto Gallery in the centre of Sodankylä.

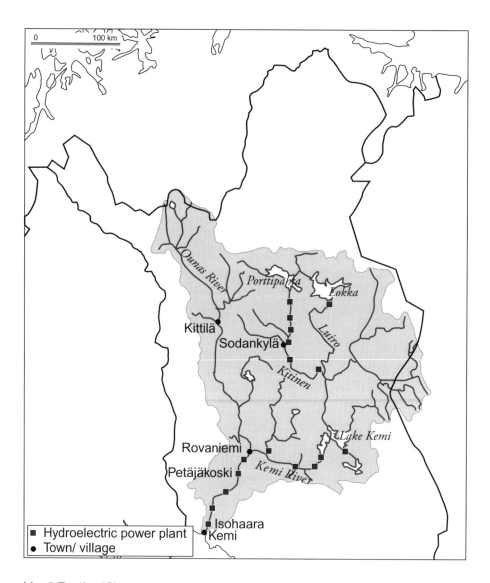

Map 5. The Kemi River water system

nineteen power stations have been built along the Kemi River, and the harnessing of its waters has seriously altered the natural environment

THE SKOLT PEOPLE

The Saamis of Finnish Lapland do not constitute a single homogenous group. One minority Saami group that has been to some extent ignored is the Skolt Saamis. They are Orthodox in religion and live mainly in Sevettijärvi, Näätämö, Nellim and Keväjärvi in the municipality of Inari. They came to Finnish Lapland after the Second World War as refugees from the villages of Paatsjoki and Suonikylä on the Russian side of the border.

In 1929 Dr. Väinö Tanner, a Finnish engineer, published a work about the Skolts *Antropogeografiska studier inom Petsamo-området* (Anthropogeographical Studies of the Petsamo Region), which has since become a classic. Tanner studied languages in Switzerland and Germany, cartography in Stockholm and geology in Russia. He taught geology and mineralogy at the University of Helsinki. From 1903 on he acquired a knowledge of Lapland by taking part in expeditions to Inari, northern Norway and the Kola Peninsula. He also headed an international commission on reindeer grazing that was established in 1909 to settle questions about grazing rights arising between Sweden and Norway after the latter had seceded from its union with the former and become independent in 1905. Tanner had also carried out surveys for mineral deposits in Norbotten in Sweden in autumn 1918. Moreover, he was a member of the Finnish delegation at the Tartu peace talks with Russia, as a result of which Petsamo became a part of Finland during the years 1920–1944.

During his surveys for mineral deposits in the Pechenga region in 1905, 1907 and 1909, Tanner had been in contact with the Skolts for years. When he first came to the area, he was told that the Skolts were lazy cheats given to drink. Tanner was in the area again in the years 1924–27, and he became convinced that these rumours were unfounded: "The Skolts are in every respect one of the most naturally talented and morally developed peoples of those we have encountered in the north."

Tanner's aim was to understand and render justice to this small people of the frontier region. The most important factor behind the way of life of the Skolts was the natural conditions in which they lived. Tanner saw their culture as

stemming from these harsh living conditions. The land and nature were the basis of everything, and the activities of individuals and communities were subservient to them. Tanner's social philosophy was probably influenced by the Skolts themselves, whose language he spoke.

When the Saamis split into different language groups, the Skolts broke up into their own sub-groups. Before the First World War, they lived in seven Lapp Villages in the Pechenga region. The Skolts differed from the Saamis living in the west in their religion, their language, their dress and their customs. Tanner distinguished three clearly different groups among the Skolts: those living along the Paats River, the Skolts of the Pechenga River, and those who lived in Suonikylä beside the Lutto River. They constituted three Lapp Villages. They lived by fishing, reindeer herding and hunting. Originally their main source of livelihood had been hunting. In the spring, those Skolts that had taken up reindeer herding followed their herds from the inland winter villages to their spring sites and from there to their summer ranges on the shores of the Arctic Ocean. When autumn came, the Skolts once more collected their belongings and headed inland to their autumn villages, where they continued their hunting and fishing activities. They returned to their winter villages in time for Christmas. During the winter they conducted their affairs with the religious and secular authorities; there were court sessions, marriages were celebrated, the local priest held services, and the older members of the clan taught the children the ancient ways and told them stories of by-gone days. When the Petsamo/Pechenga region was divided between Finland and Russia first in 1920 and then again in 1940, it meant that the traditional grazing ranges of the Skolts were split up and this led to the gradual extinction of their old livelihood. At the beginning of the twentieth century there were about 850 Skolts living in the Pechenga region. Today, at the beginning of twenty-first century, Finnish Lapland is home to around 550 Skolts.

Skolt Saami women from Finnish Lapland in 1999.

A post bus at Kaamanen in Inari in 1935. Post buses are a common sight on the roads of Finnish Lapland: they not only carry the mail but also transport passengers.

MIGRATION

After the Second World War, there was a powerful movement of emigration from Finland to Sweden. Particularly southern Sweden needed labour for its growing industry, and the people of northern Finland needed work. The emigration peaked in 1969 and 1970, when over 40,000 people left Finland for Sweden. In this respect, the position of Finnish Lapland was weak: according to an estimate made in 1970, of the thirty municipalities in Finland that lost the most inhabitants, eighteen lay in the Province of Lapland. Every municipality there apart from one experienced a loss in population. The municipalities that experienced the largest losses were Salla, Pelkosenniemi, Ranua, Posio and Ylitornio. Most of the emigrants from Lapland moved to the industrial cities of central and southern Sweden.

The situation in Finnish Lapland gave strong cause for concern, but even so in a book published in 1971 called *Lappi tänään* (Lapland Today), the provincial governor expressed confidence that Lapland would rise from "its present disfunctional trough". The structural upheaval in society hit Lapland badly. The growth of the population in Finnish Lapland had peaked in 1966, but thereafter the population curve had been downward. The population of the Province of Lapland (previously the Jurisdictional Districts of Lapland and Kemi) has grown as follows:

Year	Population
1810	17,300
1860	31,600
1920	86,700
1945	146,850
1965	211,107
1985	200,943
2005	186,386

One of the greatest skiing stars from Finnish Lapland in the 1960s was Eero Mäntyranta. He won altogether seven Olympic medals. Today visitors can learn about his achievements at the Mäntyranta Museum in Pello.

Ethnically, about 1500 members of the population in 1810 were Saamis and around 4000 in 2005. The growth of the population has gone hand in hand with changes in the number of jobs available and the structure of the economy. In the 1960s, the number of those who earned a living in agriculture and forestry began to decrease rapidly as the service sectors expanded, and in most of the municipalities of the Province of Lapland, under ten per cent of the population were any longer earning a living in primary production. Forestry began to be mechanised in the 1960s, and at the same time the so-called "set-aside" programme in agriculture also caused labour to be transferred from primary production. The situation was alleviated a little during the 1960s, at the time of the Cold War, when military garrisons were established in Lapland in consequence of the fact that Finland found itself embraced by the representatives of two great military alliances: NATO (Norway) and the Warsaw Pact (the USSR).

In the 1980s and 1990s, the population of Lapland began to fall again. The small villages of the province that had been intensively settled in the pioneer enthusiasm of the nineteenth century began to be emptied at an alarming rate of young people and concomitantly of services like post offices and schools. The abandoning of its villages was not Lapland's problem alone: the structural changes in society had affected small rural communities in a similar way all over the country. The constantly growing competition made small farms unviable, and in a globalising world there were insufficient alternative sources of livelihood that could be made available for the inhabitants. The urban centres (Rovaniemi and the Kemi-Tornio region), on the other hand, were areas of growth in Lapland. The economic crisis of the 1990s was specifically an agrarian one.

Kemi is the industrial capital of Finnish Lapland. The picture shows Veitsiluoto's sulphite pulp mill, which was built in the 1930s.

Röyttä Harbour in Tornio in 1959. Tornio is an old port through which over the centuries products from the north have been exported all over Europe. In the course of time, the original cargoes of reindeer products, butter and tar have been replaced by exports of products of the wood-processing industry and technology.

Since the Second World War, Lapland has been politically dominated by two powerful groups: the Centre Party (previous called the Agrarian League) and the Left Alliance (previously the Democratic Alternative and the Finnish People's Democratic League), which is a reflection of the region's economic and political culture. The following table shows the voting behaviour of the people of Lapland in general elections during the period 1945–2003 in terms of the percentage of votes cast:

| | AL/Cen | FPDL/DA/LA | NC | SDP | Others | MPs returned from |
	%	%	%	%	%	Lapland (women)
1945	42	28	12	14	4	8 (0)
1966	34	35	8	14	9	10 (1)
1987	38	28	12	14	8	8 (1)
2003	45	25	10	15	5	7 (1)

AL/Cen = Agrarian League/Centre Party
FPDL/DA/LA = Finnish People's Democratic League/Democratic Alternative/Left Alliance
NC = National Coalition Party (conservative)
SDP = Social Democratic Party

In the 1990s, support for the Left Alliance dropped in Lapland, as it did throughout the country along with the fall of the Soviet Union. Nevertheless, there are still traditionally strong left-wing enclaves in Lapland such as the Kemi-Tornio and Kemijärvi industrial areas, Kolari on the western frontier with Sweden and Salla on the eastern one with Russia. A workers' association was formed by sawmill and factory workers in Kemi as early as 1887. In more northern regions, the left received support mainly from small farmers, labourers and forest workers. The fall in support for the left in the 1990s was reflected in a corresponding strengthening of support for the Centre Party. The proportion of women among the members of parliament representing Lapland was among the lowest in the country throughout the twentieth century. This is partly explained by the structure of rural occupations and the cultural codes related to them. The preserve of women has been considered to be the home rather than public office. Laestadianism is another factor that has contributed to obstructing the entry of women into national politics.

CULTURAL LIFE IN FINNISH LAPLAND IN THE 1960S AND 1970S

At the same time as Lapland experienced a rapid structural change in its economy with concomitant emigration and unemployment, there arose in cultural circles a debate about the position of Lapland's own writers and artists. One of the leading voices in the debate was the writer Erno Paasilinna (1935–2000), who was born in Petsamo. He was perhaps the best-known "Lapland writer" of the day; most of his works were set in Lapland and dealt with its history and its present. By the 1960s, Paasilinna had published anthologies of essays and articles and novels. In the debate, he set out to question the antithesis "the cultural south vs the cultureless north". According to him, most of the literature dealing with Lapland from the time of Olaus Magnus in the early sixteenth century to the period following the Second World War was characterised by the fact that it regarded Lapland as an unintellectual place that was alien to culture.

After the Second World War, there were more determined efforts to develop Lapland into an area with its own culture. This polishing of its cultural image was connected with the effort to get provincial status for the region and with the programme to build a regional identity and spirit of local affiliation among its inhabitants. One example of this was the establishment in 1945 of a journal called *Kaltio*, which claimed to be "the cultural mirror of the young north". The editorial of its first number was pertinently entitled "Our Regional Cultural Heritage". It demonstrated that, despite the exceptional conditions prevailing there, northern Finland with Oulu as the cradle of its culture had "made a contribution to the intellectual life of the country that was downright astonishing"; it was just unfortunate that it had passed unnoticed in southern Finland. The aim of the journal was to promote culture in the region and to unite the efforts that were being made in Lapland, Kainuu and Northern Ostrobothnia to promote culture and the attempts to conserve valuable traditions. It did its best to support young artists and scholars, who were the lone standard-bearers of culture in the north.

ANNIKKI KARINIEMI-WILLAMO

PORO-
KRISTIINA

OTAVA

The cover of a book written in 1953 by Annikki Kariniemi, who was born in Rovaniemi. Lapland has inspired both foreign and local artists.

The activists on the paper had a huge task on their hands: Lapland had been physically ravaged and spiritually crushed. In the years immediately following the war, the region had also been culturally isolated from the rest of the country. When it got back on its feet thanks to intensive building, the construction and operation of the new power stations and extensive forestry operations, it found a new self-confidence in its cultural assets as well. The change was reflected in writings in the press which began to demand the establishment of technical schools, folk high schools and a university in the region. The University of Oulu began functioning in 1958 and the University of Lapland in Rovaniemi in 1979.

The 1960s revolution in cultural life in Lapland was reflected in the fact that a young radical like Erno Paasilinna was appointed editor-in-chief of *Kaltio* in the autumn of 1963. Before that, Paasilinna had worked on the journal since 1955 as an assistant and sub-editor. Now Lapland began to feature more prominently in the journal. Unlike his predecessors with their regional fervour, Paasilinna opposed regional separatism, which he considered an outdated and parochial policy. In his first editorial, he pointed out that *Kaltio* was published so far in the north that "you could say that it comes out beyond the back of beyond". Many other writers from Lapland likewise condemned the policy of rural conservation as provincial; instead, the cultural activists of the region should strive to make Lapland known in Finland, and hopefully beyond it.

Another important critic of culture in Lapland and ardent admirer of his homeland was Timo K. Mukka (1944–1973). Mukka's best-known work, *Maa on syntinen laulu* (The Earth is a Sinful Song) was published in 1964, when the writer was only twenty years of age. The novel describes the everyday life of a country village on the Arctic Circle and its inhabitants in the 1940s. At the centre of events are an adolescent girl called Martta and her home. The focal points of the plot are a Laestadian service in the village, Martta's pregnancy and the death of the father of her unborn child. Numerous grotesque events in the community are related in the novel, such as the carving up of an unborn calf in the womb of its mother.

Mukka's treatment of the community and his use of language were so unusual at the time that they aroused a heated debate when the book was published and again when it was adapted into a film in 1973. Many critics from the south thought that it was excessively bestial and sexually explicit. It was claimed that it gave a distorted image of Lapland. It was also asserted to be too primitive, too romantic and unintellectual. Religious circles in particular were appalled by it. On the other hand, some representatives of cultural life in Lapland claimed that the book was perfectly true to life.

Generally speaking, the aggressive criticism that Mukka's book aroused is an excellent example of how ignorant people in southern Finland were of the social and political life of Lapland. The intellectuals of the north were aggrieved by the condescending attitude of southerners; what did they know of "the nauseatingly exotic" everyday life of Lapland, as one critic described it?

A reindeer herder serving food to tourists in a *kota*. More and more inhabitants of Finnish Lapland earn their living from tourism, and reindeer herding has been replaced by tourist enterprises.

In the 1960s, there was a vigorous attempt in Lapland to promote new, more radical artists and writers as cultural "standard bearers". "We have Laestadianism, and communism, we remember the bombings of the Russians in the Winter War and the Germans' devastation of the land in the Continuation War, the enormous reconstruction and development", and despite it all the culture of Lapland had survived. Although they were opposed to regionalism, Paasilinna and Mukka became the standard-bearers of culture in Lapland at that time. Their works represented important break-throughs in the cultural revival of Lapland.

Reindeer hash and mashed potatoes

Lapland's best-known and most common dishes are all related to reindeer products, fish or wild berries like cloudberries, lingonberries, and bilberries. Reindeer hash, Lapp bread cheese, cloudberry soup, broiled salmon, dried reindeer meat, reindeer hoof soup and blood patties are everyday or festive fare among the people of Lapland. All the others are still popular, but blood patties are beginning to pass into oblivion. They are small round patties made from a dough of reindeer blood and flour with a piece of reindeer suet inside. Reindeer hash, which is made from the fore loin of the animal, is prepared in different homes and situations in different ways depending on the company and the cook. Here is one way of making a traditional Lapland dish, reindeer hash and mashed potatoes:

For reindeer hash you need:
50 g butter or other fat
400 g hashed reindeer meat
1/2 l water or beer
salt, a pinch of black pepper

Melt the butter in a pan. Cut the meat into slivers and add to the pan while still frozen. Allow the meat to defrost under the covered pan, gently turning the slivers of meat. When the liquid has evaporated, season with the salt and pepper. Allow the meat to cook and brown a little. Then add a little water or beer and simmer under cover for about half an hour.

For mashed potatoes you need:
approx. 700 g peeled potatoes
50 g butter or other fat
3 onions
2 dl milk
2 tsp salt

Boil the potatoes till soft. Pour away the water and mash the potatoes. In a separate pan, fry the chopped onions in butter until they are soft but not brown. Add milk to the onions and brink it to the boil. Add the mixture to the mashed potatoes and season with salt. Serve reindeer hash and mashed potatoes with a garnish of lingonberries.

The cloudberry, which grows on swamps, is Lapland's most famous berry. The Ranua Cloudberry Market, which has been held at the end of summer since 1974, brings people from all over Finnish Lapland to buy and sell this exotic delicacy.

6

FISHING AND GOLD PANNING

THE RISE OF TOURISM

It is possible to perceive at least four clearly distinct boom periods in the history of tourism in Lapland. In the first stage, lasting from the sixteenth century to the end of the seventeenth, the foreign travellers were mainly adventurers or members of the European nobility on their Grand Tour or government representatives gathering information and objects for their collections of curiosities. In the eighteenth and nineteenth centuries, with the advent of a new conception of science, the travellers began to include scientists who were interested in the cultures of northern climes as well as in things like the astronomy and natural sciences of the Arctic regions. Tornio and Aavasaksa Fell in Ylitornio were then the main destinations. The third boom period in tourism to Finnish Lapland was in the 1920s and 1930s and the fourth from the 1960s to the present day.

Boys fishing for trout, the delicious fish that swims in the small rivers of Lapland. In recent years Finnish Lapland has begun to be advertised as an interesting destination for summer tourism, and trekking, white-water rafting and fishing have attracted an ever-increasing number of tourists to Lapland in summer as well.

The first tourist lodge in Kilpisjärvi was built at the foot of the mighty Saana Fell in 1937.

During the interwar period, the attachment of the Petsamo area to Finland in 1920 had a stimulating effect on tourism in Lapland. In 1916 the road from Rovaniemi began to be extended north of Ivalo, and it reached Petsamo in 1931. At the same time, a new state-owned travel lodge was opened as a rest place at the half-way stage in Ivalo. Two travel lodges had already been built in Petsamo in the 1920s, and another three went up there in the following decade. In 1925 about 200 people visited Petsamo, but by 1936 the number of visitors had risen to around 14,000. Petsamo attracted heads of state, clergymen, artists, explorers, ramblers and a large number of scientists and scholars in various fields from Germany, Switzerland, France and Britain. For example, the first President of Finland, K. J.

Ståhlberg, and the Prince of Rumania visited Petsamo. The region was particularly favoured by British salmon fishermen.

Tourism in Lapland was also boosted by the rise of winter sports. The Finnish Travel Association opened several touring hostels and ski lodges there: in Pallasjärvi in 1934, Hetta in 1935 and Kilpisjärvi in 1937. A touring hostel was built in Inari in 1937. Salla also became one of the major winter sports destinations in Lapland, and the first Alpine ski slope was opened there in 1937. Ounasvaara in Rovaniemi and Pallastunturi got their own downhill slopes in the same year. Rovaniemi became the major destination for urban tourism, and a high-class hotel called Pohjanhovi was opened there in 1936.

The boom period in Lapland tourism ended with the Second World War, and it did not recover until the 1960s, when the public at large discovered the tourist resorts of Lapland. At the same time, the role of the state as a provider of services decreased; before the war it had controlled the practical side of tourism in Lapland. Now the hostels were owned by private individuals and communities. The popularity of the big ski and tourist resorts like Saariselkä in Inari, Pyhätunturi in Pelkosenniemi, Luosto in Sodankylä, and Suomu and Sallatunturi in Salla grew as tourism boomed in the 1960s and 1970s, although they had actually been built earlier than that. For example, tourism had begun in Luosto in 1949, when a small wilderness hostel was built on Luostotunturi Fell. The resort project progressed when the area was zoned for tourism in 1964. Ski slopes and a ski lift were constructed two years later, and a hotel was built in 1969. The popularity of other ski resorts like Levi in Kittilä, Ylläs in Kolari, Olos in Muonio and Ounasvaara in Rovaniemi also grew rapidly. Companies, local authorities, associations and individual persons began to build log cabins around the fell hotels in such numbers that all the major resorts in Lapland have become villages with their own post offices, restaurants and bus connections. The development of Rovaniemi as the gateway to Lapland is illustrated by the fact that the first Concorde aircraft landed there in December 1984.

Summer tourism in Lapland developed more slowly, partly because of the coolness of the climate and the midges. However, since the 1980s increasing attention has been paid to developing summer tourism. Lapland offers unrestricted access to trekkers and hikers as well as fishing holidays, canoeing safaris, gold panning courses, farmhouse holidays, and so on. The events that are organised in practically every village and town have also brought life to Lapland in summer. For example, the internationally esteemed Midnight Sun Film Festival is held in Sodankylä every year. The first festival was held in 1986, and over the years it has attracted many directors of international repute, like Samuel Fuller, Krzysztof Kieslowski, Jim Jarmusch, Jan Troell and Aki Kaurismäki, one of the best-known Finnish directors. The festival is characteristically a non-commercial, "anti-Cannes" type of event, where famous directors, film buffs and ordinary filmgoers can meet without the hullabaloo and ceremony of a typical film festival. The focus is on the films themselves, which are shown non-stop for five days and nights.

An advertisement for the 2004 Midnight Sun Film Festival. The festival has been held in Sodankylä since 1986. The provision of cultural facilities and events in Finnish Lapland began to expand in the 1980s.

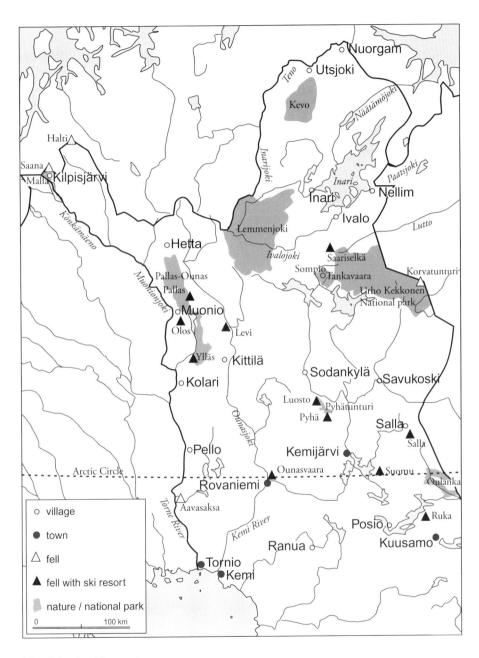

Map 6. Lapland for tourists

SALMON FISHING

Fishing is one of the most popular pastimes among summer visitors to Lapland. Salmon was the most important fish in Lapland's biggest river, the Kemi River, until it was dammed in 1949. It is also the most important fish in the Torne and the Muonio Rivers as well as in the rivers that debouch into the Arctic Ocean such as the Teno. Fish was, along with hunting, the most important source of livelihood for the pioneer settlers and Saamis who lived along the rivers until agriculture began to take a stronger hold in the nineteenth century. In addition to salmon, they caught whitefish, pike and burbot, and in the coastal parishes also vendace and Baltic herring. In the early sixteenth century, Olaus Magnus wrote: "Every shore, island, bay, river and stream offers a plethora of fish throughout the year." At that time, seals were also hunted on the coast. The major salmon fishing stretch of the Kemi River, on the other hand, was its lower waters, at the point where the fish begin their journey upstream from the sea. Salmon fishing on the Kemi River was bountiful right up as far as Rovaniemi.

Because salmon fishing was such an important source of livelihood in the large river valleys, the Crown soon imposed its control over it, and it was taxed just like other occupations. Salmon fishing registers recording the exact numbers of nets each village possessed have survived from the sixteenth century. When the town of Tornio was founded in the early seventeenth century, it caused a certain amount of conflict between the inhabitants who lived along the Torne River and the townsfolk. The size of the catches of salmon involved is indicated by the fact that in the early seventeenth century about 350,000 kg of salmon were estimated to swim up the Kemi River in the summer. At the same time, salmon fishing began to be concentrated in the hands of a decreasing number of persons, and the Crown also began to exert tighter control over it: it considered that it owned the rivers and the fish in them, and that the peasants enjoyed only an immemorial usufruct of them.

A salmon dam in the Könkämä River. Salmon was the prize catch on Finnish Lapland's main river, the Kemi, until it was harnessed.

In the lower waters of the Kemi River, salmon were caught with nets, seines, dams and hand nets. The equipment used depended on whether the fishing was done in the spring, summer, autumn or under the ice in winter. The salmon swam into fresh water at the mouth of the river as soon as the ice melted in spring. In May and June they started their migration upstream along the overflowing banks of the river, reaching the end of their journey at the end of July. They returned to the sea when the water began to freeze. The main fishing season began in early summer, when the salmon swam in the mainstream of the river after the subsidence of the floods. The fishing was done by fishing corporations, some of which were formed by villages, within strictly demarcated fishing grounds. In addition, every riverside farm had the right to practise fishing. Dams were the most effective way of catching salmon. In the 1550s, there were thirteen sizable fishing dams along the Kemi River, 26 in the 1680s, and 47 in the 1860s. They were mainly large dams extending into the middle of the river, but they remained in place only for specific periods. In addition, there were dozens of small dams on the river banks and in the flood waters; they were used during the annual spring and autumn floods. The fixed dams were kept as far as possible in the same places from one year to another, although they were often destroyed by the violent breaking-up of the ice in the spring and the heavy floods, and their locations might thus change somewhat. From the 1870s on, fishing with dams began to be impeded by the floating of logs down the Kemi River. At the same time, sea fishing came under the control of the state. Today, at the beginning of the twenty-first century, salmon fishing is still practised on the Teno and Torne Rivers in Finnish Lapland.

On the Kemi River there have been incessant disputes about salmon fishing. As late as 1979, a deputation went to Helsinki to demand compensation for losses caused by the damming of the Kemi River. This popular protest was nicknamed "The Fur-Hat Deputation" from the fur hats worn by the protesters who travelled from Lapland to Helsinki. Since then there have been several deputations of men and women from Lapland to demand due rights for their province from their "lords and masters" in Helsinki.

GOLD PROSPECTING

Interest in the mineral wealth of Lapland began in the seventeenth century during the time of Swedish rule. For example, the Kengis Ironworks was opened in Pajala on the border between Sweden and Finland in the 1640s. Several new iron-mining communities came into being in both northern Sweden and northern Norway at the end of the nineteenth century. There was also prospecting for mineral wealth in Finnish Lapland. The first nugget containing gold was found there in the village of Laurila beside the Kemi River south of Rovaniemi in the 1830s. The discovery initiated surveys for gold on the Kemi River, and in 1845 the government sent three men to Siberia to learn how to prospect for gold. Prospecting then moved to the Teno and Paats Rivers, but the results were meagre.

The first major gold seams in Finnish Lapland were found on the Ivalo river in the 1870s. The finds created a gold rush, and fortune-seekers began to pour into Lapland from other parts of Finland. The picture shows a sluice on the Ivalo River in late winter 1925. Water was directed into the sluice to flush out the mud and gravel, leaving the gold nuggets to settle at the bottom.

The search for gold in Finnish Lapland began seriously on the Ivalo River in the 1870s. At the turn of the century, the Lemmenjoki river system became the site of gold prospecting, and then in the 1930s Tankavaara in the municipality of Sodankylä. The systematic search for gold was started by Johan Konrad Lihr, the Director of the Finnish Mint, in 1868. A large nugget found a year earlier had produced new prospecting activities. Lihr's thirteen-man team included a geologist from the University of Helsinki and men who had worked in the gold fields of the Urals and Californaia. The first significant find (2 kg) on the Ivalo River was made in autumn 1869 by two sailors from Oulu, Jakob Ervast and Nils Lepistö, who had prospected in the Californian gold fields. To curb the gold fever, a decree was passed regulating gold prospecting in the Grand Duchy of Finland. Prospecting for gold was freely permitted to both individuals and corporations, but it became necessary to stake a claim with the Governor of the Province of Oulu and to pay for it. Moreover, it was necessary to pay the state a specific duty proportionate to the value of any finds made. In the first year, eighty gold mining claims were registered on the rivers of Finnish Lapland. Engaged in these activities were several Russian gold-prospecting companies that had previous experience of gold mining in Siberia. There were a few women in the prospecting groups, but it was not until 1946 that a woman owned a claim of her own.

In the beginning, prospecting was certainly beyond the means of the poor; the equipment, its transportation by horse and cart from Oulu to Kittilä and from there by reindeer and sledge on to Ivalo, provisions, building a dwelling on the claim and the workers' wages all required a fair amount of initial capital. The first dwellings were shacks covered with sods or planks. Forty of them went up on the river banks in the years 1870–75. In the summer, however, most of the workers lived in tents and wickiups. It was not until the worst gold rush waned and the fees due to the state were reduced that it became possible for ordinary locals to go in for gold prospecting.

A young gold-panner on a tributary of the Lemmenjoki River. Travellers can still try their luck at gold panning on the rivers of Lapland; there's always a speck or flake of gold to be found.

One of the brand images of Lapland is Santa Claus. As is well known, Christmas and the festivities associated with it were originally connected with the pagan tradition, but they were adopted early on by the Christian church to celebrate the birth of Christ. Santa Claus was probably originally a straw effigy, but in the nineteenth century in Finland he turned into a masked figure who brought presents. At the same time, Christmas gnomes and Christmas trees also became common there. The home of Santa Claus was defined more exactly in the 1920s: he lives on Korvatunturi Fell, on the border between Russia and Finland, a distance of 125 km from the village of Savukoski. It is also from Korvatunturi Fell that Lapland's mighty river, the Kemi, begins its 500-kilometre-long journey to the Gulf of Bothnia. The Tuuloma and the Nuortti Rivers, on the other hand, flow in the opposite direction, into Russia, where their waters debouch into the Arctic Ocean. For centuries traders travelled along them between the two countries. Thus the land of Santa Claus lies on a watershed in the wilderness and on the northern border between two cultures, a situation which has increased its mystery and fascination.

The home municipality of Santa Claus, Savukoski, was part of the greater parish of Sodankylä up till 1916. Its first inhabitants were Saamis, who lived by hunting. The first Finnish settler arrived there in the 1680s, and after that the Finnish influence in the region increased rapidly. The population was at its highest (about 2400) in the

1960s. At the beginning of the twenty-first century, the municipality had about 1500 inhabitants. Savukoski is culturally a characteristic logging community. The people of the frontier region earn their living from agriculture and forestry. Unlike the other municipalities of Finnish Lapland, a high proportion (42%) of the population of Savukoski were still living from primary production at the onset of the present century. There are still a couple of hundred reindeer owners there. In the Province of Lapland, agriculture and forestry are the source of livelihood for 6% of the population, and for under 5% in the whole of Finland. One third of the territory of Savukoski consists of nature reserves.

Apart from its numerous logging camps, the modern visitor to Savukoski will also find some restored Second World War fortifications. They are part of a fortified line called Salpalinna that began to be built after the Winter War (1939–40). It was intended to protect the country against the Soviet Union, and it extended from Virolahti on the coast of the Gulf of Finland in the south to the Arctic Ocean in the north. In Savukoski a stretch of fortifications extending 1.2 kilometres in length between the Kemi River and Iso Sarvilampi has been restored. It consists of tank barriers made of large rocks, dugouts, trenches and bunkers.

The marketing of Santa Claus and his wife, Mrs Santa Claus, in Lapland has not been limited to Savukoski; the Santa

Santa Claus is as much a part of Finnish Lapland as the reindeer and the fells. As everybody now knows, Santa lives on Korvatunturi Fell in Savukoski, from where he sets out every Christmas to deliver presents to the children of the world.

Claus legend has been appropriated to promote tourism in Lapland more widely. In 1985, Santa Claus's Workshop Village was opened just north of Rovaniemi on the Arctic Circle. Among other things it sells handicraft articles from Lapland. The idea for a cabin on the Arctic Circle was born in June 1950, when Eleanor Roosevelt, the widow of the former President of the United States, paid a visit to Rovaniemi. After the ravages of the war, practically the only thing the town had to show was the Arctic Circle. When information about the coming visit reached the town, the authorities quickly built a small log cabin and a post office on the Arctic Circle. Nowadays there is a whole village there, and in 2004 it was estimated to have received about 300,000 visitors. The latest attraction is SantaPark, which was opened in 1998. It is an amusement park with a Christmas theme, and it is located in a cave.

The state built the "Crown Station" at Kultala in the middle of the gold fields of Ivalo in the spring of 1870 to supervise and administer gold prospecting in the area. The Kultala station still exists for tourists to visit. The building was 8 x 15 metres in size, and it contained four rooms and a kitchen. In the yard, there was also a cabin for the workmen, a bakery, a cellar and an outbuilding, and there was a sauna on the river bank.

The first gold in Tankavaara in Sodankylä was found in 1935. Two gold prospectors, Niilo Raumala and Yrjö Korhonen, who moved there from Lemmenjoki, began to run courses in gold panning for tourists in 1969. After that, Tankavaara began to develop into one of the centres of gold prospecting in Lapland. In 1974, the first Finnish championships in gold panning and in 1977 the World Championships were held there.

NATURE RESERVES

Nature conservation is an inseparable part of life in modern Lapland. Indeed, some critics are of the opinion that it has gone to extremes there. Nature conservation strives to ensure that nature and natural resources are used sensibly so that in the long run they will yield the greatest possible material and spiritual benefit. The idea of nature conservation was born in Europe in the mid-nineteenth century, prompted by the rapid industrialisation and the overexploitation of the soil in Western countries.

The initial inspiration for nature conservation in Finland was perhaps a speech drawing attention to the need for it made by the explorer A. E. Nordenskiöld in 1880. However, it was not until 1938 that the Finnish Association for Nature Conservation was founded. Nature parks began to be established in Western countries in the late nineteenth century, and this aroused a debate on the need for them in Finland too. The majority of nature and national parks were established in Lapland, where they are also the largest in the country. The first Finnish nature park was Malla in Enontekiö, which was established in 1916.

A national park is a nature protection area which is intended for leisure activities like hiking, while nature parks were created to serve scientific purposes. In addition to Malla, there exist national parks in Utsjoki (Kevo) and Sodankylä (Sompio).

A young reindeer herder from Enontekiö has caught a calf in the separation of the reindeer. Next the calf will be earmarked with the symbol of its owner.

By the 1970s there were altogether seven national and nature parks in Finnish Lapland: Malla, Kevo, Lemmenjoki (established in 1956 in Inari), Sompio, Pallas-Ounastunturi (established in 1938 in Enontekiö on the border between Kittilä and Muonio), Pyhätunturi in Pelkosenniemi and Oulanka on the border between Salla and Kuusamo. At that time, there were nine parks elsewhere in Finland. Since then the number in Lapland has grown by one when the large Urho Kekkonen National Park was established on the borders of Sodankylä, Inari and Savukoski in 1983. In addition there is the extensive Kessi Wilderness Area. Altogether about

90% of the nature protection areas in Finland are located in Lapland, and they cover approximately 630,000 hectares of land.

LAPLAND'S ARTISTS AND WRITERS

Over the centuries the natural beauty of Lapland has inspired numerous artists and writers. Most of the artists who depicted the scenery of Lapland at the turn of the eighteenth and nineteenth centuries came from the south. However, even at that time many of the province's own artists were active, such as Eetu Isto of Alatornio, whose painting *The Attack* (1899) is an expression of the Finnish national movement. Another notable artist from Lapland at the end of the nineteenth century was Juho Kyyhkynen, who had studied in Paris.

One of the best-known artists from Lapland in the latter half of the twentieth century was Reidar Särestöniemi (1925–1981). Särestöniemi (original name: Kaukonen), who studied in Helsinki and Leningrad, immediately attracted widespread attention with his first exhibitions, which were held in the late 1950s. He is known for his colourful expressive depictions of landscapes and animals executed with thick daubs of paint. His pictures reveal how strongly he was inspired by the rich natural beauty and folk culture of Lapland. Initially he did not receive recognition in art circles, where he was considered a populist northern eccentric, but later his works came to be highly regarded. In 1964, Särestöniemi defined Lapland art as follows: "Art which uses the well-known characteristic symbols of Lapland, which despite their familiarity yet give expression to universal human distress – that is Lapland art." Särestöniemi saw living in Lapland as a source of wealth, but in order to develop he believed that the artist "should have the good sense to escape at a certain time". On the other hand, he also stated that the problems of the creative person were the same whether he lived in Paris, Nairobi or Kittilä. Särestöniemi said he got his own inspiration "from the north wind". After the artist's death, his studio in the village of Kaukonen in Kittilä was opened to the public as a museum; it is used for various functions, including classical music concerts.

Among the most popular male writers from Lapland during the last few decades are Nils-Aslak Valkeapää, Arto Paasilinna and Jari Tervo. Valkeapää (1943–2001), who was a primary school teacher by training, held the post of Regional Artist of the Province of Lapland in the years 1978–83. He received numerous prizes as a versatile artist who described the nature of Lapland, and he was also an activist in the Saami ethnic movement. He originally made a name for himself among the public at large as a singer of *yoik*s, and he helped to revive these traditional Saami chants. He began his literary career in the 1970s. He published poems in Saami, composed music, appeared in films and held exhibitions of his art. The best-known

Reidar Särestöniemi of Kittilä is one of Finnish Lapland's best-known painters. In English the title of this work, which he painted in 1973, means: The Clear Flood Waters of Spring Reach the Manor and Melt the Frozen Land.

of his books is an anthology of poems *Beaivi, áhčážan* published in 1988; it has been translated into several languages, including English as *The Sun, My Father*. The work, which won the Nordic Council's Prize for Literature in 1991, describes the relationship between the Saami and the surrounding environment, nature, their sources of livelihood, the different states in which they live and the majority populations. The position of the Saami as a minority people is a repeated theme in his other works as well.

Arto Paasilinna (b. 1942 in Kittilä) and Jari Tervo (b. 1959 in Rovaniemi) are gifted storytellers. Both began as journalists. Paasilinna is the Lapland writer who is best-known internationally. His works have been translated into twenty languages, including Hebrew, Russian and Japanese as well as the major world languages. Altogether Paasilinna has written 31 novels and four other works. Two of his books (*The Year of the Hare* and *The Howling Miller*) have been made into films in France, one (*The Happy Poison Cookeress*) in Germany and four in Finland.

The events in Tervo´s novels are usually located in Rovaniemi, the writer's home town. His breakthrough came in 1992 with *Pohjan hovi*, the title of which already situates the book in the north: Pohjanhovi is the name of Lapland's most famous hotel and restaurant. The protagonists of Tervo's novels are petty criminals and rascals, and their stories, lies, quips and patter are woven into hilarious stories of the way of life in the north.

Only a few of the early women artists from Lapland are known. The most famous of them was Emilia Appelgren (1840–1935) from Kemi, who studied in Stockholm. Among the best-known recent female artists and writers from Lapland are Kirsti Paltto, Merja Aletta Ranttila and Rosa Liksom. Kirsti Paltto, a teacher by profession, is a writer from Utsjoki. She has been President of the Union of Finnish Writers, and she has worked as director of a Saami-language theatre. Paltto has written books for both children and adults. She holds the preservation of the Saami language close to her heart: "I write in my mother tongue, Saami, because I know it best." Paltto draws her ideas from the Saami narrative tradition and Saami mythology. The best-known of her works is *Guhtoset dearvan min bohccot* (Dig Well, Our Reindeer), published in 1986.

Merja Aletta Ranttila was born into a Laestadian family in Karigasniemi in the

Now, at the beginning of the twenty-first century, Lapland is going through a new age in youth culture, and intriguing developments are taking place, for example, in the world of music. The Rovaniemi pop star Antti Tuisku became the pin-up of Finnish teenage girls when he was placed in the first three in the Finnish Idols competition of 2004. Young men from Ivalo and Inari like Aziz (Aslak Länsman) ja Amoc (Mikkal Morottaja) have brought a special flavour to young people's music in Lapland with their Saami-language raps. Since it is hardly possible to deal with urban street culture in Ivalo and Inari, these young men rap about subjects like the fells, the bitter winds, nature and the mystique of Lapland. They have had to invent words to describe life in the modern world. "In our language there are 150 words for snow but hardly any urban vocabulary." In addition to Ivalo and Inari, there are also northern rappers from Sodankylä, Rovaniemi and Utsjoki.

Many young women, too, have found new ways of expressing themselves and their culture through music. Tiina Sanila from Sevettijärvi in Inari performs traditional Skolt chants (*leúdd*) and sings pop rock in the Skolt language. Skolt chants are usually about animals and places, but personal chants are the best-known type of leúdd. Usually they tell of some key events in a person's life like falling in love, betrothal

Tiina Sanila (b. 1983) has inscribed herself in the history of Finnish rock music with her songs in the Skolt Saami language.

or marriage. Skolt is the most imperilled of the Saami languages spoken in Finland. Sanila and her band have made the world's first Skolt-language rock album called *Sää'mjânnam Rocks!* (Saamiland Rocks!). Despite her popularity, Sanila has no intention of becoming a full-time artiste; instead she is determined to complete her legal studies and become "a reindeer-herding woman lawyer".

municipality of Utsjoki. She comes of mixed Saami-Finnish stock. She began her work in the pictorial arts in 1980, and during the following decade she became known particularly for her powerful linographs, which are dominated by a sense of anguish and fear. She held her first private exhibition in Rovaniemi in 1988. Her works have also been exhibited in Germany, Sweden and Norway. Her pictures of that era combine exotic and mythical elements of Lapland, demons and writhing female figures. In the early 1990s, she began to produce delightful pictures of children, which have spread all over the world in the form of postcards. Ranttila has also published books for children.

Another famous artist from Lapland is Rosa Liksom (original name: Anni Ylävaara), who was born in Ylitornio in 1958. She is an artist and writer whose short stories written in the dialect of her native Torne River Valley became extremely popular in the 1980s and 1990s. In addition to writing, Liksom paints, draws cartoons and makes short films. "Writing and making art of all kinds is a way of life for me," she says. "I do this above all because I enjoy my pottering immensely."

Liksom's works deal not only with life in the remote villages of Lapland but also with the sub-cultures of the big cities. She drew her inspiration for the latter themes from the periods she spent living in Copenhagen and Moscow. Her works have been translated into French and the Scandinavian languages. Like Liksom, most modern artists from Lapland are at least as international as their predecessors. Back in the eighteenth century, French illustrators and explorers travelled to Lapland to describe and depict its nature and people, but today the artists of Lapland do this themselves and in a much more realistic way.

"LAPLAND OF THE REGIONS"

Lapland has always fascinated artists and it has also produced a large number of artists and writers of its own. In many of their works, everyday life in Lapland

The gradual building of a road network in Finnish Lapland brought the motoring middle classes to the fells in the 1930s. These tourists are seen against the scenery of the Pallas-Ylläs fell area.

is depicted as harsh and joyless against the radiating natural background. And indeed for many ordinary inhabitants of Lapland life is not easy even today at the beginning of the twenty-first century, beset as they are by powerful processes of change in the north. The exodus to southern Finland and abroad in the search for work has, among other things, impeded the development of universities in the north. However, a neo-regionalist policy which aims to decentralise decision-making power to the periphery of the country has given new hope to those who seek to develop the region.

When Finland became a member of the European Union in 1995, it meant the end of one era, which had begun with the independence of the country in 1917, and the beginning of a new one, which was characterised by a more European orientation. The regional policy which has been practised in the EU since the 1950s, and which is now at the beginning of the twenty-first century under heavy pressure for reform, also extends to the peripheral areas of Finland. Immediately after Finland joined the EU, the outlying regions of the country qualified for special support as "sparsely populated regions with a cold climate". Although the expansion of the EU may bring about a reduction in this support, the concept of "a Europe of the regions" is in any case changing the waning economy of remote areas.

The on-going reformation of economic and cultural areas of operation, the awakening of regional consciousness and through it the strengthening of regional identity are very visible in Finnish Lapland at the inception of the twenty-first century. However, another process is also visible: the area is becoming fragmented – to the extent that one can speak of "a Lapland of the regions".

Within the Province of Lapland, one can distinguish at least six economically and culturally different "Laplands". The Torne River Valley on the frontier with Sweden was the traditional "gateway to Lapland" and the common image of the north in the minds of outsiders. Central Lapland, with its fell hotels and ski resorts, developed into an independent unit of its own with the growth of mass tourism in the 1960s. Saamiland (*Sápmi*) was defined on the map of Finland in the 1980s as comprising the municipalities of Enontekiö, Inari, Utsjoki and the northern parts of Sodankylä. Other separate regions of development with their own historical and

Since the 1970s, Lapland has become a region of luxury cabins and villas. Spreading fell villages like Saariselkä, Levi and Luosto, offer skiers dozens of groomed slopes, après-ski activities and snowmobile safaris. However, some visitors prefer the peace of nature and build their own cabins in the shelter of the forests. The picture shows a cabin beside the Jeesiö River in Sodankylä.

cultural characteristics are Rovaniemi and its environs, the Kemi-Tornio industrial area and the eastern Lapland district.

The development of Finnish Lapland will depend on specialisation. The keys to success will be the inhabitants' awareness of the multicultural history of their region and the strong local expertise engendered by it together with cooperation between the North Calotte and Barents regions and other actors in Europe.

SOURCES

This book is mainly based on the author's own works. In addition, the works mentioned in the following list of references have been used. For further information about Finnish Lapland, see also http//www.lapponia.net

CHAPTER 1.

ULTIMA THULE

Julku, Kyösti, ed. **Faravidin maa. Pohjois-Suomen historia**. Oulu: Pohjoinen, 1985: 82–200.

Kehusmaa, Aimo. Kivikausi ja varhaismetallikausi. **Faravidin maa. Pohjois-Suomen historia**. Ed. Kyösti Julku. Oulu: Pohjoinen, 1985: 10–42.

Koivunen, Pentti. Esihistorian loppujaksot. **Faravidin maa. Pohjois-Suomen historia**. Ed. Kyösti Julku. Oulu: Pohjoinen, 1985: 50–74.

Kulonen, Ulla-Maija, Irja Seurujärvi-Kari and Risto Pulkkinen, eds. **The Saami. A Cultural Encyclopaedia**. Helsinki: SKS, 2005.

Lähteenmäki, Maria. *Kotini on vanha siida*. **Suvaitsevaisuus. Suomalaisen ja saamelaisen Lapin rajankäyntejä keskiajalta nykypäivään**. Ed. Mikko Lahtinen. Helsinki: Tanner-Akatemia, 2001: 52–68.

Olaus Magnus, Gothus. **Pohjoisten kansojen historia**. Suomea koskevat kuvaukset. Helsinki: Otava, 1974.

Pihlaja, Päivi Maria. *The Study of the North in the 18th century. Knowledge of Lapland in Europe, and Its Significance for Foreign Scholars*. **The North Calotte in Perspectives on the Histories and Cultures of Northernmost Europe**. Eds. Maria Lähteenmäki and Päivi Maria Pihlaja. Publications of the Department of History, University of Helsinki 18. Inari: Puntsi, 2005: 25–37.

Schefferus, Johannes. **Lapponia**. First edition 1673. Hämeenlinna, 1979.

Seurujärvi-Kari, Irja, ed. *Beaivvi Mánát. Saamelaisten juuret ja nykyaika*. **Tietolipas 164**. Helsinki: SKS, 2000.

Taylor, Bayard. **Northern Travel: Summer and Winter Pictures of Sweden, Denmark and Lapland**. New York: Putnam, 1858: 80.

Teerijoki, Ilkka. *Tornionlaakson asutuskehitys*. **Tornionlaakson historia II. 1600-luvulta vuoteen 1809**. Jyväskylä: Gummerus, 1993: 11–44.

CHAPTER 2.

THE BIRTH OF FINNISH LAPLAND

Kulonen, Ulla-Maija, Irja Seurujärvi-Kari and Risto Pulkkinen, eds. **The Saami. A Cultural Encyclopaedia**. Helsinki: SKS, 2005: 199–203.

Lähteenmäki, Maria. **The Peoples of Lapland. Border Demarcations and Interaction in the North Calotte 1808–1889**. Helsinki: Finnish Academy of Science and Letters, 2006.

Lähteenmäki, Maria. **Kalotin kansaa. Rajankäynnit ja vuorovaikutus Pohjoiskalotilla 1808–1889**. Helsinki: SKS, 2004: 15–33, 50–51, 109–128, 212–221, 346–365, 448–458.

Lähteenmäki, Maria. *Suomen Lapin synnystä alueiden Lappiin*. **Terra** 117.3, 2005: 147–158.

Snellman, Hanna. *Women Working Their Way Through Logging Camps*. **The North Calotte. Perspectives on the Histories and Cultures of Northernmost Europe**. Eds. Maria Lähteenmäki and Päivi Maria Pihlaja. Publications of the Department of History, University of Helsinki 18. Inari: Puntsi, 2005: 136–147.

CHAPTER 3.
THE LAND OF SAAMIS AND SETTLERS

Annanpalo, Heikki. **Aikain muistot. Lapin kuvauksia neljältä vuosisadalta.** Helsinki: Edita, 2000: 105–109, 158.

Enbuske, Matti. *Peräpohjolan keskusseudulla.* **Rovaniemen historia 1721–1990.** Jyväskylä: Gummerus, 1997: 173–299.

Hyne, Cutcliffe. **Through Arctic Lapland.** London: 1898: 97, 271.

Lehtola, Veli-Pekka. **The Sámi people: traditions in transition.** Inari: Puntsi, 2002.

Lähteenmäki, Maria. **Kalotin kansaa. Rajankäynnit ja vuorovaikutus Pohjois-kalotilla 1808–1889.** Helsinki: SKS, 2004: 240–269, 313–320, 403–428.

Lähteenmäki, Maria. **The Peoples of Lapland. Border Demarcations and Interaction in the North Calotte 1808–1889.** Helsinki: Finnish Academy of Science and Letters, 2006.

Lapinmaan komitean mietintö 3/1905. Helsinki: 1905.

Paasilinna, Erno. **Laaja Lapinmaa.** Hämeenlinna: Karisto, 1965: 320–328.

Paulaharju, Samuli. **Lapin muisteluksia.** Helsinki: WSOY, 1922.

Paulaharju, Samuli. **Taka-Lappia.** Helsinki: WSOY, 1927.

Pennanen, Jukka and Klemetti Näkkäläjärvi, eds. **Siiddastallan. Siidoista kyliin.** Inarin saamelaismuseon julkaisuja 3. Oulu: Pohjoinen, 2000.

Strode, Hudson. **Finland Forever.** New York: Harcourt, 1941: 147.

Strohmeyer, Curt. **Im Zauber Suomis.** Berlin: Deutschen verlag, 1939: 22.

Suomen sotasurmat 1914–1922. http://www.narc.fi

Turi, Johan. **Turi's Book of Lapland.** London. 1931: 34–35.

CHAPTER 4.
FINNISH LAPLAND IN THE SECOND WORLD WAR

Annanpalo, Heikki. **Aikain muistot.** Helsinki: Edita, 2000: 179–180.

Junila, Marianne. **Kotirintaman aseveljeyttä. Suomalaisen siviiliväestön ja saksalaisen sotaväen rinnakkaiselo Pohjois-Suomessa 1941–44.** Bibliotheca Historica 61. Helsinki: SKS, 2000.

Lähteenmäki, Maria. *Ett marginellt norden? Det finska Lapplands ställning från 1920-till 1940-talet*. Historisk Tidskrift för Finland 4/2001, 561–578.

Lähteenmäki, Maria. **Jänkäjääkäreitä ja parakkipiikoja. Lappilaisten sota-kokemuksia 1939–45**. Historiallisia tutkimuksia 203. Helsinki: SHS, 1999.

Lehtola, Veli-Pekka. *"The Right to one's own past", Sàmi cultural heritage and historical awareness*. **The North Calotte. Perspectives on the Histories and Cultures of Northernmost Europe**. Eds. Maria Lähteenmäki and Päivi Maria Pihlaja. Publications of the Department of History, University of Helsinki 18. Inari: Puntsi, 2005: 83–167.

Nyyssönen, Jukka. *Stepping across the borders – the Finnish elements in the identity politics of the Samii Litto*. **The North Calotte. Perspectives on the Histories and Cultures of Northernmost Europe**. Eds. Maria Lähteenmäki and Päivi Maria Pihlaja. Publications of the Department of History, University of Helsinki 18. Inari: Puntsi, 2005: 95–107.

Paasilinna, Erno. **Kaukainen pohjola**. Hämeenlinna: Karisto, 1968: 266–278, 292–304.

Paasilinna, Erno. **Maailman kourissa**. Helsinki: Otava, 1983: 172–181.

Tuominen, Marja. *A Good World after all? Recovery after the Lapland War*. **The North Calotte. Perspectives on the Histories and Cultures of Northernmost Europe**. Eds. Maria Lähteenmäki and Päivi Maria Pihlaja. Publications of the Department of History, University of Helsinki 18. Inari: Puntsi, 2005: 148–161.

Ursin, Martti. **Pohjois-Suomen tuhot ja jälleenrakennus saksalaissodan 1944–45 jälkeen**. Rovaniemi: Pohjois-Suomen Historiallinen Yhdistys, 1980.

CHAPTER 5.

POWER STATIONS AND RESERVOIRS

http://www.rovaniemi.fi/lapinkavijat/vaeltaja/historia/htm/

Kerkelä, Heikki. *Teollistuva Lappi osana maailmantaloutta*. **Lappi. Maa, kansat, kulttuurit**. Eds. Ilmo Massa and Hanna Snellman. Helsinki: SKS, 2003: 129–159.

Lappi tänään. Helsinki: WSOY, 1971.

Linkola, Martti, ed. **Entinen Kemijoki**. Helsinki: Weilin & Göös, 1967.

Lähteenmäki, Maria. *Pohjoiset reservit. Lappi kuvina ja mielikuvina 1960–70-luvun kulttuurikeskusteluissa*. **Historiallinen Aikakauskirja** 3/2001. Helsinki: Suomen Historiallinen Seura: 233–245.

Lähteenmäki, Maria. The Finnish regional policy in Lapland in 1945–95. Lecture delivered to the NorFA Conference, the Barents Region Network, Archangelsk, Russia. 20.9.2005.

Lähteenmäki, Maria. *Villi ja vapaa Pohjola. Kansantaiteilija Andreas Alarieston mennyt maailma*. **Suomi. Maa, kansa, kulttuurit**. Eds. Markku Löytönen and Laura Kolbe. Helsinki: SKS, 1999: 184–197.

Porotieto. Rovaniemi: Paliskuntain yhdistys, 1994.

Snellman, Hanna. **The Road taken. Narratives from Lapland**. Inari: Puntsi, 2005.

Statistics Finland. Parliamentary elections 1945–2003.

Statistics Finland. Population 1945–2005.

Tanner, Väinö. **Antropogeografiska studier inom Petsamo-området**. Helsingfors: 1929.

CHAPTER 6.
FISHING AND GOLD PANNING

Arvola, Oiva. *Luovan ihmisen vaikeudet – Reider Särestöniemen haastattelu* [an interview with Reider Särestöniemi]. Kaltio Febr/1965.

Haveri, Arto and Asko Suikkanen. *Lapin aluekehitys ja sen tulevaisuus*. **Lappi. Maa, kansat, kulttuurit**. Eds. Ilmo Massa and Hanna Snellman. Helsinki: SKS, 2003: 160–182.

http://www.rosaliksom.com

http://www.rovaniemi.fi/lapinkirjailijat.htm

Jauhola, Satu. **Merja Aletta Ranttila. Oma kuva**. Inari: Puntsi, 1999.

Kumpulainen, Jarkko. *Nupit koilliseen*. Kaltio June/2004.

Olaus Magnus, Gothus. **Pohjoisten kansojen historia**. Suomea koskevat kuvaukset. Helsinki: Otava, 1974.

Paasilinna, Erno. **Maailman kourissa**. Helsinki: Otava, 1983: 108–115.

Partanen, Seppo J. **Sankareita, veijareita ja huijareita. Lapin kullankaivajien tarina**. Helsinki: Edita, 1999.

Ruotsala, Helena. **Water regulation and local inhabitants: a study of ecological refugees in northern Finland**. Finnish-Hungarian Symposium on Ethnology. Budapest: Hungarian Ethnographic Society, 1993: 99–118.

Suopajärvi, Leena. *Ympäristöpolitiikka ja luonnonsuojelu Lapissa*. **Lappi. Maa, kansat, kulttuurit**. Eds. Ilmo Massa and Hanna Snellman. Helsinki: SKS, 2003: 183–199.

Vilkuna, Kustaa. **Lohi. Kemijoen ja sen lähialueen lohenkalastuksen historia**. Helsinki: Otava, 1974.

PHOTOGRAPHS

City of Rovaniemi 101

Finnish Defence Forces 81, 89, 90

Leuku Photo Agency:

11/Jorma Luhta, 31/Pekka Antikainen, 39/Arto Liiti, 50 Marja Pirilä, 73/Paavo Hamunen, 97/Pekka Antikainen, 106 above/Pekka Antikainen, 116/Pekka Antikainen, 117/Jorma Luhta

Maria Lähteenmäki 119, 122, 128, 141

National Board of Antiquities 21, 37, 45, 106 below/A. Pietinen

Otava archives:

18, 23, 26, 34, 41, 47, 48, 52–55, 57–59, 61, 63, 65, 68, 69, 74–75/Eino Mäkinen, 77, 78, 87/A. Pietinen, 94, 99 both, 109, 110 both, 114, 120, 125/A. Pietinen, 127, 133, 139

Studio Tunturi-Lappi/SKOY 131

Särestöniemi Museum 135

Maps: Johanna Roto

INDEX OF PERSONAL NAMES